Our Energy Matters

The Art of Crystal Reading

Learn How to Manifest Your Heartfelt Intentions

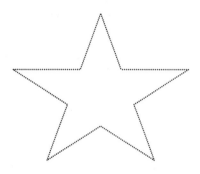

"Think good thoughts not bad.
Life is too short for feelings of fear and hate.
And when your life is over, you will be able to say,
'I have lived a life worth living'! "

Dena Marie
Age 11

This book is dedicated to the child who never stopped dreaming

Edited by Wayne Warren
Copy Editor: April Gleave

Graphic Design by Dena Marie and Wayne Warren

Photography by Dena Marie

Printed by :
Snohomish Publishing Company Inc.
605 2nd Street
Snohomish, Washington 98290

Distributed by Dena Marie

* Special thanks to James Waneless for his permission to use the images from the Voyager Tarot and to Doreen Virtue for the use of her words of wisdom from the Archangel Oracle Cards.

Acknowledgements

My heartfelt love and thanks go out to my three children , Charissa, April and Michael. They are my shining stars and my greatest teachers. To my husband Wayne, my best friend, my wizard, my knight and my guiding light! Thank you for always encouraging me, to be me. I love you all every minute!

To those of you, who have done your homework. You are beacons of light to others and have inspired me to push on. Thank you for the cards, the unexpected calls and gifts that fed my spirit in times of uncertainty. Most of all I thank the Stars, the Angels, my Guides, the ones who have crossed over before me and Blessed Mary. Thank you for the synchronicities that have been scattered along my path, guiding me home, back to myself.

There is no place like home (Ohm)…

"May the facades we wear,
fall to the earth and scatter to the wind, never to be seen again!"

Dena Marie
Age 43

Table of Contents

Introduction

Socrates said, "know thyself," and Plato added, "The life which is unexamined is not worth living." This sums up my motivation to share what the universe has taught me. I once had a client say, "Do you know how hard it is to be yourself?" It should be the easiest thing we do, to slip comfortably within ourselves, but some how we have been energetically manipulated into denying the core part we call "I." Isn't that what we are all searching for, ourselves? Crystal Readings are a way to discover more of yourself and the people you care about. I am still amazed at how much I know about an individual when they draw their crystals, and I am in awe when these simple techniques take a person to a higher level of knowing. It feels as though I reintroduce my clients to their forgotten selves. That is what these readings are truly all about.

Over many years, the Art of Crystal Reading has been slowly revealed to me by something beyond my own intelligence. Like so many others, I feel we have forgotten much of what we've learned thousands of years ago when our wisdom and our knowledge of ancient teachings were so much deeper. I call it *re-membering*. Uncovering this information can be an enlightening experience. This manuscript is an accumulation of hundreds of books I have read and contains a similar amount of knowledge that has been revealed to me while meditating, running or simply while I was driving down the road. The universe is always *re-minding* us of who we really are and leading us back home to our source. We just need to be more conscious of how this information is communicated. Dreams, synchronicities, nature and everyday metaphors are all ways the Divine Mind speaks to us. Can you fathom the lesson that the salmon have been trying to teach us? Instinctively, they have always returned to their source where life springs anew, but recently in our history, this cycle has been broken. Our own source is our ancient wisdom. By understanding this knowledge, you really can become your own psychic, in a sense. Tuning into your higher self, listening to *your* inner voice and taking action can be easy when you know how and have been given guidance. After all, who knows you better than you?

Increasing your knowledge about yourself can only lead to a more harmonious life… a healthier life. My goal is to empower others to participate in their own healing. If during a reading you could see what diseases (blocked energy) were manifesting in your body at that very moment, would you take the extra step to heal yourself? Teaching others to take that step is my vision, encouraging them to invest more time and resources in themselves. Loving and caring for yourself can have such a positive influence on your health. Prevention of disease, rather than treatment, is the most effective step we can take toward achieving a vital and healthy lifestyle. Simple things like vacations, extra time with loved ones and doing what makes you happy, will lead you to wholeness. Also, if you feel healthier, the world around you will benefit as well. Taking small steps toward healing yourself will touch all of the people you surround yourself with, as well as the rest of the world, on a collective unconscious level. It could be called the "trickle up, down and all around theory!"

"If you bring forth what is in you, what you bring forth will save you. If you do not bring forth what is in you, what you do not bring forth will destroy you."
-Jesus *The Gospel According to Thomas*

How it started

As far back as I can remember, collecting crystals has always been a passion of mine. Like a kid in a candy store, I would touch and admire their beauty. I was first drawn to stones like amethyst and rose quartz. Now, I have hundreds in all shapes, colors and sizes, worn in earrings, necklaces and rings. I feel that each stone has certain properties and influences. For instance, if I need to be grounded, I will wear a darker stone like obsidian, to bring me down to earth. If I want to be more intuitive, then I will wear an amethyst. When situations call for courage and strength, I keep tiger's eye close by. If I need to speak up for myself, I will wear turquoise around my neck, and to love myself, I will wear a rose quartz necklace close to my heart. When I decided to share my fascination with crystals, I gave them to my friends, family and coworkers. The children I encountered seemed to appreciate the stones most, and would treasure the crystals I gave to them.

I believe that when we invest positive energy into our keepsakes, they brighten our day and shine blessings down upon us. Like a four-leaf clover or rabbit's foot, I have heard many good luck stories about the crystals I have given as gifts. My favorite story is about one of my son's friends who found it difficult to hit a baseball and would always bunt. One day before a game, I took him and my son to the batting cage. I gave him a power stone (tiger's eye) and asked him to focus on hitting the ball. That afternoon he not only hit the ball, but continued to hit the ball all season long. He kept the stone in his pocket, and throughout the games, it gave him confidence and power. We all need to feel powerful, but we all need to be loved as well. I like to pass on rose quartz to a lot of women friends of mine as an occasional reminder to love and nurture themselves, just like a string tied around their finger.

Crystal Readings began while traveling with my family. I would buy loose stones at "new age" bookstores, and keep them in my car's ashtray. The very first reading I did was with my children. I was trying to entertain them in the car while we waited, and they became bored and restless. I told them each to pick their favorite "rocks." As time went by, this came to be known as the "rock game." I had been reading books for years on the chakras and their corresponding colors, and I knew the meanings of each color and what each crystal represented metaphysically. Connecting these ideas is what started the evolution of my art.

My collection of crystals began to overflow and spill onto the floor of my car with every turn, so I started asking passengers to pick their favorite and take it with them. I would take note of which stones were drawn, and what it told me about the individual. My oldest daughter is very bright, imaginative and strong-willed. She would always choose the dark purple amethysts and yellow tigers' eye stones. She has a natural psychic ability and very vivid dreams, and her choice in crystals seemed to agree with these characteristics. The amethyst's purple signifies intuition and imagination, and the yellow and black tiger's eye is the stone that represents power and control. My younger daughter is very loving and giving, almost to the point of being sacrificial. With her heart being so open, she was consistently drawn to feminine rose quartz. My girls were total opposites and the stones they chose always reflected that.

As the *rock game*'s significance started to increase, it began to resemble a psychic reading. When I started playing it, I had people pick only a few stones. Later in its progression, I decided that people should choose seven of their favorite stones, representing the seven main chakras. This gave me insight into a person's chakra-related characteristics. This transition gave birth to what I now call "Crystal Readings." To my amazement, even when I performed readings on complete strangers, their accuracy never failed. As years went by, my children asked me do readings with their friends. After a reading, I would know more about the people my children chose to spend time with, which worked in my favor most of the time.

Being a single mother of three and having little time for myself, I knew more balance was needed in all aspects of my life. Surprisingly, I found I could perform the readings on myself. On many stressful days, I would choose the crystals that called out to me. Sure enough, they would reveal what chakras were being neglected. My stones consistently revealed that I was not grounded and that my head was in the clouds. I was always losing my keys, talking too fast and was in constant motion. My prescription was to take time to slow down and nurture myself, to get more sleep and to make time for play allowing me to get back into my body. Taking that extra time getting to know myself paid off through the years and made life more enjoyable.

The more I did Crystal Readings for others and for myself, the more I noticed that they would show signs of blockages in the energetic body. I would look at the crystals and ask if anything was going on in that area and they would comment on some correlating illness. If the crystals revealed blockages in their throat I would ask if anything was going on in that area and they would respond with "I just had my tonsils taken out." If I asked about their heart chakra they might respond with comments regarding asthma or blood pressure issues.

It was becoming clear to me that the unseen energy that works within us all ultimately determines our physical health. This intangible energy field that flows through our chakra system is the most important indicator of our over all health. Chest and back pain, sore throats, headaches and ulcers would be seen in the individual's crystal layout, indicating to me that energy blockages stop the universal life force energy, slowly depriving our bodies of needed vitality. I believe our thoughts and emotions have a profound affect on the way our body's function. While I believe our energy affects our health, I also believe our thoughts affect our energy systems known as chakras. Interpreting the crystals to discover emotional and energetic imbalances was a hit or miss process for a while, but after a lot of practice the mind/body connection was added to my readings.

Over the years my Crystal Readings grew into a more diversified experience, incorporating the mind/body connection and several other aspects such as numerology, astrology, and a lot of intuition. Colors and the chakras were the basis of my readings but as my hunger for metaphysics grew, the methods of my readings changed accordingly. I added Tarot cards years later after taking a Spiritual Counselors' course. I usually have my clients pick a card when I feel we need verification in the direction the reading has taken. Most sets of Tarot cards will contain a book with them; I have each person read directly from the book after choosing a card… it works wonderfully. At the moment, I've added more than just Tarot to my readings. My current readings end with the drawing of an Angel card; I call them the "fortune cookie" cards. I also recently added numerology. Using numerology can reveal where you are in your life cycle. Cycles show us that there is a time to begin new ventures; work hard, and a time to reap what you have sown. This bit of information can add to the reading significantly. When I am finished with a reading, I give them a small bright piece of paper with a chakra prescription and a crystal to take with them as a reminder of what they need to do as homework. I call myself an "Energetic Counselor" and have incorporated my Crystal Readings into my professional practice. I find that Crystal Readings help me pinpoint core issues more efficiently, saving a great deal of time and money for my clients. I have written this book because I've discovered, over hundreds of readings, that you don't have to be Einstein to realize that our **energy matters**.

"Every stone is Light, slowed down and tied in a knot; and Light is every stone's dream."
-Robert Alexander

As I look back on the evolution of my art, I can see its slow and natural growth into its current manifestation. Over a fifteen-year period, I have done hundreds of readings on friends, family and many people I have never seen before. The readings that I did with new acquaintances were the most revealing and have strengthened my belief in my newfound art. To introduce you to the connection between all of the methodologies I will introduce in this booklet, I feel it is best now to give you a brief example of a reading I had performed many years ago.

I did a reading with a man from Alaska, who was in town for an operation on his left shoulder. His condition told me he was having issues with a woman and they were weighing down on him (mind/body). In his reading, I saw that he was missing his power and throat stones (chakras). He chose four stones representing his heart chakra, one was a faded pink, two dark green and another was green and black (colors). The green and black stone suggested to me that there was pain in his heart caused by a male in his life. Malachite was one of the crystals in his heart chakra; it encourages expression of feelings and empathy with others (crystals). The pink faded stone suggested a female was also involved. Being the energetic detective that I am, I asked him if he had a heart-felt issue with a woman weighing on him that he needed to discuss, and if he had lost control or felt powerless with a male in his life. I explained the energetic blocks that I saw in his chakra system. Without hesitation, he opened up to me (throat chakra) telling me his son had been murdered and that he and his wife had never been able to talk about it. He desperately wanted to express the pain and heartbreak that he had felt after losing his son in such a horrific way, but his wife never wanted to discuss it, that explained the left shoulder operation. I saw that both of them were water signs (astrology), holding back emotions would have been exceptionally detrimental to their marriage and to their health. His wife had become a workaholic and was headed for some health-related issues of her own. My prescription for him was to open communication with his wife. He did so in a very sincere letter… and last I heard they were doing fine. If I had practiced numerology at the time, I would have expected to see the couple in a 1 or 2 year cycle, informing me that they would have to start over again and take their relationship to the next level.

As you make your way through this book, I will help you understand the chakras, colors, crystals, astrology, numerology, mind/body connection and most importantly, your intuition!

"All truths are easy to understand once they are discovered; the point is to discover them."-Galileo

The Chakras

The word chakra means "wheel" in Sanskrit, an ancient East Indian language. There are seven of these major energy centers in the human body (and hundreds of minor ones) and they receive, assimilate and distribute energy throughout our energetic fields (auras). Each chakra is unique and has its own individual characteristics and functions, all of equal importance. These seven energy systems resonate and vibrate at the same frequency as their respective colors of the rainbow, and are the network through which the body, mind and spirit can come together. Chakras are energy vortexes (discs) that distribute universal life force energy throughout the body. This life energy or "prana" flows down through the top of your head (the crown chakra), through your spine, to your pelvic floor (the root chakra). The root chakra is the color red and has a very dense earth vibration, whereas the upper violet crown chakra vibrates at the highest frequency. When energy flows evenly through each chakra we achieve optimal health. I like to think of the chakras as spinning discs connected by an energetic hose, working together in our own synchronized bio-computer. When one or more discs fail to spin, become bogged down, overloaded or damaged, the other components will try and compensate and the whole system will suffer. All these components need to work in synch with one another in order to maintain balance in our bodily and spiritual systems.

When we are judged or ridiculed, and not appreciated for our differences, we shut down our chakras and shift into a mode of *surviving*, instead of *thriving*. A great example is a child growing up in a non-communicative home. If the child asks too many questions, talks incessantly and is always moving about, a frustrated parent might say "sit down", "shut up" and "quit asking so many questions." If this message is played repeatedly, the child will stifle his self-expression and inquisitiveness, resulting in blockages in the throat and upper chakras. This manifests in the body as a sore throat, headache or ear and eye problems. Eventually, the child ceases to express himself. His teacher from school may write home, "your child never asks questions in class and is extremely timid." Reading this, the parents are dumbfounded, asking "how could our child, who is such a chatterbox, not ask questions in class?"

Flash forward to adulthood. The child, now fully grown, works in an office and he is afraid to talk to his boss about a great idea he has that will save the company millions of dollars. He gets anxiety attacks just thinking of standing up and talking at meetings. When he thinks of opening his mouth he feels paralyzed, he wants to talk to his boss but an unknown force holds him back in his chair. This persistent fear arises from a typical chakra imbalance that may lead to oral fixations such as smoking or overeating to ensure he keeps his mouth **shut**.

How can we remedy this? It is a two-step process. First, we identify the issue by finding the blocked chakra. Second, we develop a prescription to remedy it. In the example of the boy with a stifled throat chakra, we might suggest that he express himself through writing, drama, or even Karaoke on a Saturday night! Understanding what causes blockages will enable us to make the appropriate changes, giving us back our power and vitality. Increasing our knowledge about ourselves and doing something different can get us back on track. Those of you with blockages in your throat chakra can do so much more than the Karaoke in our example. You could take voice lessons or attend a class on something you enjoyed doing when you were a child. You could ask the teacher easy questions and reignite the inquisitiveness you had earlier in life. For your "chakra opening" graduation, you could spontaneously stand up and sing at your friend's birthday party and ask them how old they are.

Of course, all this could have been avoided if we were allowed to be our true selves from birth, and emote with freedom. Energetically, we were all born into this world as perfect and unique individuals. We did not come here to conform and be like anyone else. We are here to fulfill our purpose and live our lives according to our own personal missions. Live written backwards spells *evil*. My definition of *evil* is not being true to oneself. It is never too late to be born again and become our own parents, giving ourselves everything that we need to truly LIVE!

In the following chapters, I'll discuss many types of blockages and prescriptions, which can remedy the kinks. Each chakra, like the one in our example, responds to different stimulations. No matter where your blockage manifests, there is a healing action you can undertake.

"When I'm trusting and being myself as fully as possible, everything in my life reflects this by falling into place easily, often miraculously."— Shakti Gawain

Our energetic stairway to heaven

The first chakra is located at the base of the spine and the seventh located at the crown of the head. They all correlate with certain parts of the body, colors, elements and lessons. When a chakra is too open or blocked, it is associated with certain *dis-functions* of the body. Chakras that are too "open" are a direct result of compensating for "closed" or blocked chakras. For example, a blocked fifth (throat) chakra could result in a fourth (heart) or sixth (third eye) chakra which is too open. Open or blocked, the state of each chakra reflects the decisions we have made in our lives, and how we choose to feel and respond to our past conditioning. When the chakras are balanced, you live a life of health and ease. When imbalanced, you live a life of *dis-ease*.

The first or root chakra deals with grounding, survival, and the contact between our bodies and the physical world. The colors representing this chakra are red and black. It is located at the base of the spine. The feet, ankles, legs, rectum, adrenal glands and large intestines are all associated with this chakra. The corresponding element is earth, and the chakra's related lesson is discovering our connection with mother earth and with our physical bodies.

The first chakra will be associated with fear, money issues, addictions, and low self-esteem. If the chakra is too open – one might manifest bullying, becoming overly materialistic, feeling self-centered, exhibiting violence, or becoming greedy. If this chakra is blocked, we may have low self-esteem, or become emotionally needy and self-destructive. When it is healthy, we belong; we are stable, secure and patient. We are also able to release the past. If it is unhealthy, an inability to let go of negative emotions manifests, leading to obesity, hemorrhoids, constipation, and sciatica. Having stability in our lives is a sign of a healthy first chakra. If we are changing jobs and moving all the time, we may find it difficult to have a foundation to build upon. Without stability within ourselves, dependable relationships will elude us and we feel alone, unsupported and unloved as a result. We may have weight issues and self-destructive habits that take the rug out from under us. Treating our body with the respect it deserves and loving our true inner self is essential for optimal health. Self-love starts here; we cannot have healthy relationships if we cannot take care of ourselves. We can only attract into our lives what we already know to be true within ourselves. Thus, the first chakra is the beginning!

The second or sacral chakra is located at the lower abdomen and is connected with family, relationships, sexuality, feelings and reproductive life. The sacral chakra is all about connecting with other people. It is associated with emotions, fluidity, nurturing and union. The color is orange and the element is water. Physically, it relates to the reproductive system, the urinary tract, the womb, testes, ovaries, lower abdomen, kidneys and prostate plexus. Its lesson is sharing, intimacy and communion with others. If it is blocked, we are emotionally unbalanced, manipulative, sexually addictive, jealous and over indulgent. If it is too open we become over-sensitive; we also feel guilty for no reason and can easily be controlled by others.

A healthy second chakra helps us feel connected with others - we are giving, passionate, harmonious and spontaneous. If it is unhealthy, we become disconnected, frigid, impotent, and resistant to change. We may have infertility, reproductive disorders and lower back problems. Movement and adaptability are most important in forming relationships with others. The second chakra is about relating with others yet maintaining our personal boundaries. We change, adapting and flowing like water moving throughout the land. Trusting another, being able to ask for help, and holding nothing back, allows us to commit to relationships that test us and challenge our fluidity. When we play it safe and cease to relate with others, we will find our second chakra blocked.

When we fail to join with others in our own child-like way, we will feel alone and desolate, as if being surrounded by a barren desert. Surviving alone is not enough; we need relationships to maintain a whole and healthy existence. Flexibility and the will to open ourselves to change, helps us merge and grow with others. If in our past we have been hurt or abused by someone we have loved and trusted, we may shut our second chakra down to protect ourselves emotionally. With accumulated past family disconnection, we may keep ourselves isolated in fear of being hurt again. Yet, we can still join outside groups, and clubs that become our surrogate families. Pets are also a wonderful way to share a connection and keep the sacral chakra healthy. Supportive relationships are a must in moving up to the next empowering chakra.

The third or solar plexus chakra is located in the upper abdomen. It is associated with the ego, personality, willpower and metabolism. The color is yellow and the element is fire. The stomach, digestive system, pancreas, gall bladder, liver and small intestines are the physical areas of this chakra. The lesson from this chakra is learning to come from a place of power and strength, projecting who we truly are.

This chakra is the chakra that forces you to be you. When the solar plexus chakra is healthy, we live purpose-filled lives, and exhibit self-control. We are radiant, warm and life is a joy. If it is unhealthy, we may have digestive and eating disorders, diabetes or ulcers. When this chakra is in a healthy state, we can become powerful outside our homes, and we can move in a path that is aligned with who we truly are.

When this chakra is too open we may feel angry, controlling, judgmental or obsessive. If it is blocked, we feel insecure, afraid, powerless and overly concerned with what others think. If you grew up in a house where you felt like a stranger and lacked approval, or felt weak, you might have issues with self-empowerment! Anger, tears and regrets are stored under this chakra when it is blocked, and stomach disorders and anxiety are the result. Lacking self-control results in eating disorders and is a powerful way to say, "I want control of my life and I will find that control, even if it is self-defeating." Always doing for others and second-guessing yourself is a symptom of an out-of-balance third chakra. Ask yourself "what do **I** want?"

When we think poorly of ourselves and entertain negative thoughts, we may find it difficult to pick ourselves up and continue on life's journeys without the encouragement and support from friends and family. Without the boost of our healthy relationships we may lose momentum in our own evolution. Moving up our stairway of chakras allows us to access energy centers of higher and higher vibration. However, each step must be solid in order to climb to the next. Adhering to this idea, we can maintain a healthy third chakra only if we have stability and supportive relationships. Otherwise, it is like building a castle on sand. Furthermore, honoring yourself, having discipline and self-respect will help you move with conviction toward the center of the chakra system.

The fourth or heart chakra is located in the center of the chest. Its element is air and the colors are green and pink. The heart chakra is associated with divine unconditional love, forgiveness, compassion and understanding. The physical areas are the heart, lungs, breasts, thymus, circulatory system, arms and hands. The lesson of this chakra is to learn to forgive and love yourself and others unconditionally. If it is too open, we will feel sacrificial, wounded, overly dramatic and unworthy. If it is blocked, we love with conditions, are possessive, feel unbalanced and become repressive. When the heart chakra is healthy, we are motivated by love, experience peace, and feel content. When it is unhealthy, physical effects can manifest such as heart disease, asthma, and circulation problems, as well as lung and breast related issues.

A healthy heart chakra says:
"I have built my foundation."
"I have relationships with people I love, and I love myself."
"I am ready to serve and be part of all of humanity."

The term *sacrifice* might come to mind when thinking of this chakra. However, altruistic action is driven by the belief that we are all one and the same - if I do for you, I do for all. Even a simple smile to a stranger can lift all of humanity. The phrase "do unto others" takes on a whole different meaning knowing that we are all cells in the same body. All of our actions have effects that reverberate throughout the networks that we experience everyday: our family, our friends, those we simply meet on the street, and thus the whole world. Since we are all joined together in this way, we cannot afford to have disconnection, or even worse, "individual (dividing) cancerous" cells, destroying the harmony of the collective human energetic body we call "God."

Joining with others means experiencing the emotions that go with such connections, good and bad. Letting in the joy means also exposing us to feeling vulnerable. The ebb and flow of happiness, grief, compassion, and pain are the necessary dance of an open- heart chakra. Anyone who feels dissociated from others may have heart-related issues. Stopping the flow of emotions in life may cause heart attacks, strokes, autoimmune disease and blood pressure issues. High and low blood pressure is an indication of how much of life's heartaches you are holding onto, or how much you are willing to release.

The heart chakra is also a storage vault and the gateway for past emotional pain such as grief. We tend to force feelings down and they accumulate… until something menial happens. Like a volcano, we can erupt. To emote, literally means to move. Releasing trapped emotions involves forgiveness, and the insight needed to see the pain that holding onto these emotions may cause. Forgiveness truly means "giving forward", enabling you to let go of the repressed emotions from the past that may be weighing you down and holding you back from living a healthier today. *The past, is the past, can we get past it?*

The fourth chakra is of the utmost importance because it is in the middle of the seven-chakra system. It connects the physical to the spiritual and is related to healing. Clearing this chakra and keeping it healthy will insure a life filled with light and love, helping you in your next progression toward the chakras of the ethereal world.

The fifth or throat chakra is located in the neck area, the color is turquoise and the element is sound. This chakra is associated with free expression, communication, and the will to make your voice heard. The correlating physical parts of the body are the throat, shoulders, mouth, thyroid, parathyroid, neck, teeth and gums. This chakra's lesson is knowing who we are and having the confidence to express ourselves to others. If the throat chakra is too open, we are over-talkative, dogmatic, self-righteous and have lack of discernment. If it is blocked we are indecisive, hold inconsistent views, repress expression and lack personal power.

When this chakra is healthy we are communicative, honest, reliable, creative and loyal. If it is unhealthy we have sore throats, gum disease, teeth, neck, thyroid and speech problems. True communication comes from an ability to transmit and receive information through a verbal or written exchange - expressing our internal dialogue or inner voice with the limited choice of words we have in our vocabulary, and enabling us to honestly share ourselves with others. There is nothing more frustrating than trying to express your self to another person and not be understood. Clear communication with yourself and others comes with practice, patience and understanding.

A healthy fifth Chakra says:
"I freely communicate to others my personal choices and desires."
"I know who I am and what I want in life."
"I am willing and able to express my visions to others."

The fifth chakra represents self-knowledge that is communicated to others. Holding back your words, unable to speak up for yourself and lying to yourself and to others, shuts this chakra down. Creative pursuits empower this chakra: singing, art, poetry, and writing. Choosing our own expressive outlets allows us to freely communicate our most precious gift to the world, ourselves. Reaching ever upwards toward the stars, we float into the next chakra!

The sixth or *third eye* chakra is located in the middle of the forehead and the colors are indigo and purple. It is associated with light, intellect and consciousness. It is the seat of intuition and imagination. Physically, it represents the brain, nervous system, nose, ears, sinuses, left eye, hypothalamus and pituitary gland. The lesson for this chakra is to live in the present moment guided only by your inner knowing. If this chakra is too open, we become spaced out, overly analytical and we live in our heads. If it is blocked, we lack imagination, cease to dream and become much too logical.

When this chakra is healthy, we are intuitive, focused and clairvoyant. When it is unhealthy, we may suffer from a lack of concentration, headaches, nightmares, blindness and deafness. The sixth chakra is stimulated by disciplined imagination, such as visualizing yourself becoming healthier or landing that promotion that you always wanted. Seeing your life goals and dreams come to fruition into the physical world are certainly good signs that your third eye is working properly. It is also a sign that you've been listening to your inner voice. Some of us will deny this voice and falter, becoming a staggering mirage of who we are truly meant to be.

We shut down our sixth chakra when we question or doubt the strong inner voice that says "this feels right for me." We sell ourselves short when we do not realize how wise and powerful our inner voice truly is! There are physical consequences for neglecting your intuition. Migraines and eye problems result when we choose to deny our inner sight, and our hearing may fade when we cease to hear our inner voice. We also throw our sixth chakra into disarray if we have to block out something painful that we've seen in our past. Nightmares can manifest when we force thoughts away that are too painful, forcing us to clean out our mind's computer of unwanted programming while we sleep. Working through painful issues before they create disease in this area can be difficult at first, but the reward is well worth it. One cannot put a high enough value on peace of mind and clarity. Your intuition or inner knowing is your most powerful tool in living a healthy and happy life. If you flex your intuitive muscles, they only get stronger and can help guide you back to where you came from: your spiritual source.

The seventh or crown chakra is located above the top of your head; it is light violet or white in color and represents thought, spirit and the divine. Enlightenment and oneness with the infinite are this chakra's lessons. The physical areas are the top of the head, pineal gland, right eye, central nervous system and upper brain. If this chakra is too open, we become confused, frustrated, overly attached to outcomes and extremely sensitive to light and sound. When blocked, we lack inspiration, feel alienated, depressed and worried. When this chakra is healthy we live in the present, are connected with the divine, live purpose-filled lives and are equanimous. When unhealthy, we become exhausted for no apparent reason, feel lonely and we seem to lack purpose.

The seventh chakra says
"I have an idea, and with intention, I will manifest it into the physical world."

The seventh chakra connects us to the ethereal; this is where we integrate our individual soul with the life force of the universe. It is through this connection that we are able to manifest our purest thoughts from within our imagination into this dense world of matter. With conscious thought we can create our world, choosing peace of mind, clarity and neutrality. The physical world is the screen to our inner mind's projector, manifesting our thoughts and perceptions for all to see. As Jesus said, "ye are gods." We are the co-creators of our own reality. We are spiritual beings living in the physical world. This is precisely the reason our intentions are so important; they are truly our thoughts (prayers) waiting to manifest into the physical world. By being consciously connected to our higher selves, each of us can become aware of the divine plan and express it in our own individual ways. When we know our purpose and hold a pure vision of that idea, then we are using the gift of visualization as the "Divine Mind" intended. By holding this vision within our highest chakras (meditation), it guides us into realizing our full potential and re-minds us, "On earth as it is in heaven." Inspired, or *in spirit*, we are moved to envision, create and be uniquely ourselves. Who am I? I am I… Everything else is just an illusion!

"The enlightened man…whose consciousness embraces the universe, to him the universe becomes his 'body,' while the physical body becomes a manifestation of the Universal Mind, his inner vision an expression of the highest reality…." -Lama Anagarika

Manifesting Heaven on Earth

When it comes to manifesting our intentions into this physical world, we engage in a process of bringing energy from the universe into our crown, and down through our bodies, engaging each chakra in the process, eventually giving birth to our ideas… landing heaven on earth. An idea starts as a seed of energy. When this life force energy flows downward and into our bodies, it starts with an "aha" moment. We become inspired through the crown chakra. Everyone has seen the familiar picture of a light bulb above a cartoon character's head. Imagine that this is exactly what the crown chakra would look like when turned on. With our sixth chakra open we begin imagining the idea and we begin to play it out in our mind's eye. If it seems plausible, we then express the idea to another person or simply write it down. At that moment, our idea is out of our head and becomes manifested in the "real" world. Feeling a strong heart-felt desire, we push it forward, or shall I say, downward into our power chakra. Remember that the third chakra gives us the drive to manifest our true vision and the motivation to make it happen. By using our willpower, we get things done, creating and working with others. These personal connections engage the second chakra. We then give birth through the first chakra, grounding our idea into physical form. Then a new thought "pops" into your head and the whole process starts over again.

Let's take a look at the whole process using an example. You have an "ah ha!" moment that you may want to buy a new home. You have a vision, you see the house in your imagination, you talk it over with you realtor; you feel the need to have it, and work extra hours for the down payment. You shop with your spouse and find the home of your dreams, buy it, and move in. It seems easy, but what happens when we have a chakra blockage? We may end up hitting a wall at some point in the process. Maybe you have third chakra issues, and you don't want to work the extra hours. If you have first chakra issues you may spend the money on something frivolous before you buy the house of your dreams or actually manifest the house and then not make the payments. If you have sixth chakra issues you may not have the ability to see yourself in a new home in the first place. Remember that we are spiritual beings in a physical world; therefore everything starts out as an intangible idea in the ethereal realm. You cannot produce anything pure in this world without your intentional thoughts. Clear up your chakras, and your every wish is our universe's command!

"Energy and persistence, alters all things." -Benjamin Franklin

Examples of "Blocked" or "Too Open" Chakras

Steve Stuk can't seem to keep a job. He lives with his parents and lost his driver's license due to unpaid speeding tickets. He feels stuck and can't seem to motivate himself to do anything other than sleep all day. When Steve was younger, his family uprooted and moved every year. He never felt like he could get attached to anyone at school so he learned to play alone. Steve feels his parents owe him and he blames them for all his problems in life. Steve has a blocked first chakra.

Samantha Sympathetic volunteers at her church, her children's school and the women's mission. She has a hard time saying "no," and feels guilty if she does anything for herself. When she was younger her parents argued about money. When she needed anything for school she would never ask her parents and learned to go without. She wished she could fix her parents and that they would change, but she is often disappointed. Samantha has a much too open second chakra.

Sid Vishus likes to play to win. If he loses, he gets very angry. Most people won't play games with him because of his temper. Once he attacked one of his coaches at school after losing a game. Sid grew up unsupervised, with five older brothers who teased and tormented him. He learned early on that if he held in his tears, his brothers would leave him alone. Sid's third chakra is too open.

Harry Heartless purposely says things that make people cry. He feels satisfaction at his job when he makes the big deal, even if someone else has done all the work. When Harry has a bad day, he likes to take it out on his family, including the dog. Harry's mom died tragically when he was only ten years old. He swore he would never feel that way again and he said he would never forgive god for what had happened. Harry has a blocked fourth chakra.

Kathy Chatter loves to talk. She calls her friends and can speak to them for hours on the phone. She likes to gossip about her friends and neighbors. She knows she does it but can't stop herself. Her husband doesn't talk much. She complains about her husband constantly to her family while he is in the room. Kathy felt ignored by her parents when she was younger. They had a lot of family problems and didn't have time for chit chat. There was no communication in the home unless it was to criticize. Kathy has a fifth chakra that is too open.

Danny Daydreamer loves to live in his head. He imagines all the money he will have when he wins the Lotto. He sits for hours each day, pondering what he will do with all that money. He goes to his job daily but never finishes his work because his head is in the clouds. Danny was an only child who spent too much time alone. He liked pretending that he was somewhere else. He never wanted to go outside and play. Danny's sixth chakra is too open.

Debbie Downer is always alone and she feels depressed most of the time. She worries all day and night, she has a poster of Murphy's Law in her office. Her coworkers pity her and invite her to social functions, but when she goes, she brings everyone down. Debbie was an orphan and was raised in foster care. Every time she got her hopes up to have a family they were smashed. She never did get adopted. "Why bother," is her mantra. Debbie has a blocked seventh chakra.

We all know people who have great ideas, but sit at home and do nothing. We also know many people who refuse to look into the future and don't dare to dream. These are a few common examples of chakra *blockages*. Our energetic potential is always pushing at these gates trying to manifest our wishes into the "real world." Blockages may arise in response to various sources of stress and struggle in our everyday lives. A person could be raised in an unloving atmosphere, and the result could be a blockage in their heart chakra, which could possibly develop into heart-related problems. Moreover, one could also spend time in a very oppressive environment, leading to a shriveled power chakra, which can lead to many eating disorders. As children we may have been full of imagination and creativity, but when expressing that vision to someone else, we were silenced with the words "What a stupid idea!" Such feedback obviously stifles one's creative expression in the throat chakra. We are products of our past, but remember, the past is behind us. Becoming conscious of our blockages allows us to make the necessary changes to heal our past and become whole and free-flowing individuals again.

When "grounded" in your first chakra, you can accomplish tasks that start from your sixth and seventh chakra's thinking processes and your mind's imagination. By incorporating your throat chakra, you use discernment, and creativity, driven by positive emotions in the lower heart and power chakra. With your second chakra spinning evenly, you can obtain the desire and support needed to manifest your dreams into reality. Learning to love and respect yourself could literally save your life… and think of all the money you could save in doctor bills! Healthy successful people live balanced lives. They realize that ALL chakras are equally important, and like muscles, atrophy when they are not exercised. The chakras, when at ease, flow and give birth to all your ideas. After all, that is why we are here, to live a fulfilling life and manifest spirit into physical form.

The Chakra System in Our World Today

Another way to understand the chakra system is to know how it influences our everyday situations. For example, the other day I received an email on the plight of the polar bears. It seems that through global warming they are drowning in the Arctic Ocean. There is not enough prey to feed on, so they must swim longer distances to survive. The polar ice has been melting, giving the bears fewer places to rest. So, when they need to catch their breath on the ice during their long swims there is nothing for them to climb upon and they drown. I listened to the thoughts racing through my mind as I progressively reacted to the news:

- *My first reaction was fearful*: "We are all going to die in a flood!"
- *My second, emotional*: "How stupid are we humans?"
- *My third, empowering*: "Wait, what can I do to help? I can stop driving my car."
- *My fourth, community connected*: "I can lead a group that educates the world on the plight of the polar bears and global warming."
- *My fifth, expressive*: "I will communicate to everyone that the polar bears and ourselves are connected and by saving them we would be ultimately saving ourselves."
- *My sixth, insightful*: "I will imagine and visualize a solution to save the polar bears."
- *My seventh, all-knowing*: " I accept with equanimity that everything is perfect in this school called life!"

You may notice that my reactions marched right up through each chakra, ringing true to their characteristics as they went. From fear based "fight or flight" to divine acceptance, we can see examples of this behavior in everyday life. These examples can illustrate which chakra is most active and even unfold the process of thoughts traveling from one chakra to another right in front of our eyes. In the chakra system there are three feminine (yin) and four masculine (yang) chakras. The heart chakra being the most powerful, the altar connecting spirit and matter.

- First chakra is masculine: fight or flight
- Second chakra is feminine: emotions and sensations
- Third chakra is masculine: power and worldly success
- Fourth chakra is feminine: community and selfless service
- Fifth chakra is masculine: flow and expression of oneness
- Sixth chakra is feminine: inner knowing and conscious awareness
- Seventh chakra is masculine: pure awareness and cosmic consciousness

Today you could say that the violence in our country represents the first chakra... and other phenomena can be attributed to the rest of the chakras:

- The media and sensationalism – the second
- The war in Iraq – the third
- The United Nations – the fourth
- Bono of U2 educating the masses about Africa's AIDS epidemic through music – the fifth
- The new or "old" age movement being remembered – the sixth
- Gandhi, who represented loving peaceful resistance and equanimity - the seventh

Perceptions change depending on what level you are coming from in the chakra system. No chakra is better then any other, all of them are equally important. There is a time to run (a lion chasing you), to surrender (rehashing the past with your spouse) and a time to speak out (peace rally). There is also a time to reflect (watching a sunrise) and give it up to a higher power (pray for peace around the world) all are useful in different situations depending on which chakra you are coming from. The trick is to think of yourself as a musical instrument, keeping your chakras perfectly in tune with one another, creating balance and harmony. If one or more chakras are off key, it will affect the way your instrument will sound, so constant tuning of your instrument is encouraged.

"Yes" or "No" Questions to ask about the chakras

Asking theses questions can identify what chakra needs the most help. If there are a lot of "no" answers in more than one chakra, you then need to look at the crystals chosen and prioritize what block needs to be dealt with first. These "yes" questions represent chakras that are 100% open and healthy.

1st Chakra- earth, grounding, security, self
Do you spend time outdoors?
Are you satisfied with your chosen profession?
Do you do some type of physical activity daily?
Is your bank account in the black 100% of the time?
Do you feel safe and secure where you live?

2nd Chakra- water, fluidity, sexuality, relationships
Is your body flexible?
Are you surrounded by supportive and trustworthy people?
Is your house a home?
Do you embrace change?
Are you comfortable with expressing your sexuality?

3rd Chakra- fire, energy, will, personal power
Are you full of energy throughout the day?
Do you feel confident around people you don't know personally?
Do you finish projects to the end?
Can you be assertive when necessary?
Are you able to both laugh and cry spontaneously in life?

4th Chakra- air, love, connectedness, group consciousness
Do you love yourself just as you are today?
Are you able to forgive and let it go?
Do you feel connected to everyone around you?
Can you give unconditionally to yourself and others?
Can you, without thought, reach out and touch somebody in need?

5th Chakra- sound, communication, creativity, true self-expression
Do you communicate well, balancing talking and listening?
Are you creative in any art form?
Is your voice loud and clear for everyone to hear?
Do you express yourself freely without holding your words back?
Can you openly communicate how you feel with others?

6th Chakra- light, intuition, imagination, soul realization
Do you have vivid dreams that you can remember?
Do you rely on your intuition when making decisions?
Are you able to imagine new possibilities as solutions to problems?
Do you have psychic experiences?
Is your life filled with meaningful coincidences? (Synchronicities)

7th Chakra- thought, inspiration, equanimity, oneness with the infinite
Do you feel a strong spiritual connection with something outside yourself?
Do you frequently have good and original ideas?
Are you good at thinking in words, symbols and concepts?
Can you still your mind/meditate?
Are you consciously aware of your divine purpose?

Energy Exchange, the Chakras, and You

When giving readings, it is important to understand where your responsibility lies as the reader. I have read a few individuals where the first chakra was the only one that I could see that was functioning. The reading was all about fear, worry and survival. I felt a deep sadness for them and knew my personality was getting in the way. You can only offer up the information that comes through and the rest will be up to them. Our responsibility as the reader is to know when to let it go! I have learned many valuable lessons in not becoming too invested in the outcome of the reading or getting emotionally involved. It is important that I personally do not obstruct the natural flow of information coming through. Metaphorically, the safety tip of the oxygen mask on the plane comes to mind, you have to put it on yourself first, and only then can you assist others. Never give yourself away or you too will be living entirely in the first chakra!

"God, grant me the serenity to accept the things I cannot change, the courage to change the things I can, and the wisdom to know the difference." –Reinhold Niebuhr

Our Energy Matters

The heart chakra is very powerful, and has many sides to it. It is important to love and care for others… but loving yourself is a prerequisite to healing those around you. In order to help others, you have to take care of yourself first. When I heard about the passing of Dana Reeves, Christopher Reeves' (Superman) wife, I finally got it! Our energy really does matter. She passed away at 44, just ten months after being diagnosed with lung cancer following her husband's death, even though she was a non-smoker. I knew intuitively and metaphorically (mind/body connection) that she loved her husband so much that she had been "breathing" energetically for him for ten years after his tragic riding accident that left him paralyzed from the neck down and unable to breathe on his own. I also knew that she was a singer and entertainer but had given it up to stay with her husband and give him 100% of her time[1]. Without conscious connection with our own inspiration, we only have so much universal life force energy to give away before we deplete ourselves completely. We have to take the time to feed our spirits (oxygen mask) then we can give to others. Taking a little time for yourself can refuel you energetically so you can continue to assist the ones you love.

Self-love is associated with the heart chakra, and its color is pink. If we take care of ourselves first, then we can move up to green, where we can focus on healing others. There is a fine line drawn between the two colors (giving and receiving), and the key is balance. One of the most memorable readings I have ever done was with two women who came separately and then later had a Relationship Reading together. One of the women was a warm-hearted motherly type and the other had a cold stoic outlook on life due to a block in her heart chakra. The motherly woman was trying to work on some power issues (3rd chakra) and the other was working on healing her heart (4th chakra). They were energetically attracted to one another and, on the surface, it looked like a good thing. In the Relationship Reading, you could see that they were learning something from one another.

The woman with the blocked heart chakra had many health related issues in her throat and heart areas, some had been life-threatening but these issues were now in remission. I could see that one woman was feeding off of the other's motherly energy. The question was, could she afford to give up this energy? I thought not, especially since she had some pronounced power issues. I was in conflict, personally. I wanted to warn her, but intuitively, I knew it is not my place to do so. The words the "wisdom to know the difference" came to my mind. I let it go, and I hoped that I would get to read them again. They came back for individual readings after six months. I could tell that the woman with the motherly heart was still energetically giving herself away to save the other. She drew five pink and magenta heart stones, all tainted, and they represented childhood trauma with a woman. The stones were nothing like the previous reading. I asked her if she thought that she might be overcompensating for her friend's energy deficit. She said, "No" and I let it go.

Less then a year later, the warm-hearted loving motherly woman died of cancer that started around her heart and throat chakra. What a beautiful spirit, she taught me so much about energy and how vital it is! After the first reading with her friend, the big-hearted woman sent me a card she had made with a picture she had taken of their relationship reading. It is the only time that someone has ever taken a picture during a reading. After receiving the card, I placed it in my "helpful people" corner (Feng Shui) with the other notes and gifts from my thankful clients. When I heard that she had passed away, I got the card out and looked at it again. The card was done in pink and had a heart sticker inside. She thanked

1   "Shock As Dana Reeve Dies At 44." <u>March 7,</u> 2006. CBS News, Associated Press. http://www.cbsnews.com/stories/2006/03/07/entertainment/main1376216.shtml

me for the reading and said that she realized that everyone who walks through her door was taken care of except her… after seeing the card again I had peace of mind. The cards she chose in the picture were *purity*, *breakthrough* and *hello from heaven*. Her friend's cards were *stagnation*, *oppression* and *divine order*. Everything happened just as it was supposed to, for "the world is a perfect place including our dissatisfaction with it and our attempts to change it."

I had seen this type of energy exchange before, usually in readings with parents and their children. These Relationship Readings usually reveal that the children are trying to energetically compensate for their mother's or their father's unresolved issues. I have seen this situation with my own children over and over again. During a time in my life when I was extremely angry, one of my own children overcompensated for my aggressive energy with an overly open heart chakra. When I was flighty and spaced out, another became my "rock." There would be times I couldn't think clearly and had too much on my plate. That is when my oldest would come to my aid. As a result, her higher chakras would overcompensate while I gave mine a rest.

The ability to open and close chakras is valuable in protecting our energetic health, but over time it can cause *dis-ease* if this exchange of energy goes on for an extended amount of time within a family. Your energetic body never forgets the feelings associated with the stress whether it was yours or it belonged to some one close to you. Eventually something gives way when you least expect it, a memory, a smell or a familiar face, forcing you to deal with your past and the emotions that where nicely tucked away for a later date. Something has to give energetically in the chakra system to get the emotions flowing, moving energy through. Sometimes, this occurs more like a dam exploding versus a river flowing naturally. These "bursts" often occur with conditions that are associated with repressed emotions! Our society might call this Post Traumatic Stress Disorder (PTSD).

Most people will deal with their past when they find themselves in a safe environment. These buried emotions show up when you least expect them to, metaphorically "popping" the emotional cork in our overloaded energetic bodies. Children can also develop chakras which are too open when they act like sponges, absorbing and taking on emotions that are not their own. Blockages occur when children live in homes that are less than loving. They will shut down their heart so they do not feel pain, or they will close their third eye so they do not have to see or hear conflicts going on in the home, which may result in the child having nightmares. While adults can separate themselves from people and situations that are emotionally volatile, children do not have that option. These children can develop a blockage in the heart chakra, stopping the flow and creating an overcompensating yellow chakra that is too open… making them sick to their stomach and possibly constipated. As adults, they find they must shove their feelings down (heart burn) until a spouse, boss, or family member pushes their buttons and an emotional explosion takes place. Readings can reveal such buried energy and correct the blockage before such an outburst. Exercise such as running, crying to a sad movie, journaling or watching a funny comedian could start clearing up many stagnant trapped emotions. I have found that discussing buried pain with another person clears up most issues. Readings help discover blockages and open up communication to start the healing process. Our children, and even our pets, do what they can to energetically protect the ones they love. Eventually they become drained and they manifest their own *dis-ease*. I have seen people hold onto painful experiences, only to have their pets go to the veterinarian in pain because they cannot pass what they have eaten, or cancer arises in areas associated with the very chakra that is closed in their owners.

We all transfer energy to one another, especially between parents and their children. What we call hereditary can be merely energy passed down again and again. If a parent does not deal with their issue it goes to the next generation…it is crystal clear to me, heal yourself and you will heal your children! I have done readings for three generations, and what I have revealed has been astounding. Working with the whole family is the best way to heal a household and the experience becomes such a blessing.

The Chakras and the new (old) age

I have spoken with many breast cancer survivors and they often tell me, how difficult it is to give to themselves. Many of them are massage therapists, nurses, hospice workers and counselors, giving so much to others but unable to find time for themselves. I see them coming together in large numbers as a band of sisters - healing and loving one another. The irony of it all is that the symbol so many charitable foundations and breast cancer survivors choose to unite under is the pink ribbon, the color for self- love in the heart chakra. I also find it ironic that the color of the ribbon for supporting our soldiers at war (a band of brothers) is yellow, the power chakra directly under the heart! In the near future, I see these two polar energies blending together bringing about balance to create what I call "eggnog yellow" represented by yellow citrine and pink rose quartz - merging feminine and masculine energy into one, as yin and yang, moon and sun, god and the goddess. "The lion will be laying with the lamb" representing a strong and yet gentle loving heart, bringing about balance.

"When the power of love overcomes the love of power, the world will know peace."
- Jimi Hendrix

On occasions I will intuitively see the past lives of my clients, especially if those lives are relevant to the reading (chakras closed by past life trauma and or abuse). For example, I have seen many individuals with past lives connected with the Inquisition. Those who found the strength to fight back during that dark era in our history have practiced the occult for many lifetimes and have kept the mystery teachings well hidden. When introduced to The Art of Crystal Readings, these individuals seem to catch on very quickly, taking back their power and healing themselves in the process. Those in the past, who lacked the fortitude to fight back, watched the ones they loved be tortured and killed. In subsequent lifetimes, these women and men found themselves retreating in to monasteries until it was safe to return to the "old world" healing practices. Now these souls are back in numbers to turn the tide, reintroducing the importance of feminine healing energy into our world today. I am sure that I am one of them. What else would be compelling me to write these words and encourage others to heal themselves? I can guarantee that when I was younger (in this lifetime), I was not brought up with any of this knowledge, but it rings true from the core of my being. We can't allow our society to sedate us and silence our voices any longer! We must have the courage and conviction to speak our minds and take back our power. Let's leave the fighting behind, learn from our past, and love one another, truly moving our energy up into the heart chakra from which the Christ consciousness of compassion and forgiveness arises.

One last comment on this subject: have you ever noticed if you turn the yellow and pink ribbons sideways they look like the Piscean fish on the back of Christians' cars? Feminine and masculine energy unknowingly side by side, a new age is dawning, the age of Aquarius.

The pre-Christian history of the fish symbol: The fish has been used worldwide as a religious symbol associated with the Great Mother Goddess.

"If the fishes (Pisces) is ruled by the archetypal motif of the hostile brothers, then the approach of the next Platonic month, namely Aquarius, will constellate the problem of the union of the opposites. It will then no longer be possible to write off evil as the mere privation of good; its real existence will have to be recognized. This problem can be solved neither by philosophy, nor by economics, nor by politics, but only by the individual human being, via his experience of the living spirit..."

-Carl Jung

"It is of importance that you realize that today something new is happening. There is the emergence of a new kingdom in nature, the fifth kingdom; this is the Kingdom of God on earth or the kingdom of souls. It is precipitating on earth and will be composed of those who are becoming group-conscious and who can work in a group formation. This will be possible, because these people will have achieved a self-initiated perfection (even if relative in nature) and will be identified with certain group expansions of consciousness. It will also be because they have arrived at love of their fellowmen, just as they have loved themselves in the past. Think on this with clarity, my brothers, and grasp, if you can, the full significance of this last sentence...."

-Alice Bailey

The Chakra Cheat Sheet

On the back cover of this book is a **Chakra Cheat Sheet**. Use it in your readings as a guide. Sit with your loved ones and see for yourself how our energy matters. When I do a reading with someone close to me, I can see why we are energetically drawn together. In everyday life, these insightful interactions rarely happen between two people. I have done readings with my children and have grown with them as a result. In the future, I envision a world full of books and games that educate us about our energetic systems, aiding us in *re-membering* who we truly are! Hours of soulful entertainment, lifting our spirits and raising the collective energy of the whole! Can you imagine how differently we would have viewed life if only we had been taught this information as children? We would have established boundaries with the people around us, protecting our own energetic systems, our core selves. Loving others and ourselves equally, knowing when we were being drained of our most precious resource, ourselves. If you read this book and walk away with the understanding that you are an energetic system interacting with other energetic systems, then my job is done. Everyone and everything you encounter is energy. Our energy truly does matter! How much energy you have is entirely up to you.

"And what is man without energy? Nothing-nothing at all!"   -Mark Twain

Colors and Chakras

To understand the chakras and their related colors, I use a tree as a metaphor: Imagine your roots deep in the dark black earth, emerging from the ground through rich red and brown soil. Your stable brown trunk, protected by orange bark, supple yet strong. The yellow sun shinning down on the tree for growth that leads to bright green foliage, oxygenating the air. Your sun-drenched leaves reaching towards the bright blue sky and an indigo heaven, being fed energetically by white starlight representing the crown chakra. If you have ever visited Sedona, you have experienced this meditation fully. The colors are so vibrant, the red earth, the dark amber cedar trunk and the gold sun shining down on the greenery of the trees. Under the turquoise blue sky by day and at night a deep purple canvas above, complete with the luminous gaze of a full moon. Mother Nature displays the color of the chakras for all to see and experience, if only we can stop long enough to feel the connection.

The Observant Reader's Clues: Chakras, Colors and Personality

I observe the person I am reading from the moment we say hello. Taking note of the color of a client's jewelry or clothing, gives me clues before we even begin. People who choose to wear black tend to be protecting themselves (1st chakra), turquoise means that they feel the need to be heard (fifth chakra), while green is worn by under-cover healers (fourth chakra) and yellow is the worn by social butterflies (3rd chakra). Observe their preferences and dislikes, for everything says something about the individual. I can know what chakras may need some TLC simply by asking a client their most favorite and least favorite colors. Watching children draw with crayons is a great way to get practice. Take notice of which colors they choose to create their drawings with (adults too).

When picking their stones, I watch what colors they struggle with or put back. Even though they were not chosen, these crystals can still provide valuable information because the colors were attractive in the first place. If they go for a yellow tiger's eye and put it back, then I know they have power issues, whether or not they keep the stone. Purple stones like amethyst say "intuitive" to me, while orange has an emotional character and grey signifies depression. They often will pick eight stones, and I always hold on to the last crystal chosen and put it to the side. It can reveal what direction they are headed, or what future changes they are pondering making. The meaning of the colors will look obvious with practice, but it is important to observe carefully before jumping to any conclusions.

When reading children, I often find that the reading will not be accurate with the parents in the room. Unconsciously, the child may still be seeking the approval of their parents. This will affect their actions in the reading. For example, I was on vacation when I saw some crystals in a gift shop. I noticed a young boy choosing all blue lapis crystals, and I asked him to pick one out for my collection. I thought he would choose a blue crystal, but as soon as his father walked away he chose a large magenta one with black specks and handed it to me quickly. He was choosing the blue lapis stones to please his father, but deep inside he had a big heart and was very sensitive. That crystal is now being used in my readings, and when picked, it will indicate issues about being true to yourself.

"To thine own self be true…" -William Shakespeare

Colors

Knowing the chakras and their colors will be the very first thing you will need to learn to perform Crystal Readings. Colors have their own specific meanings correlating to their respective chakras. For instance, I see yellow and I feel joy (third chakra). Pink makes me feel mellow and in love (fourth chakra), while brown feels earthy (first chakra) to me.

I know some men who think pink (heart chakra) is feminine but continually pick pink in their readings because their hearts have blockages. If the heart chakra needs healing, I can guarantee that all preconceived stereotypical notions of society will fall away in the participant's mind. If the heart chakra is blocked the crystals will reveal it! You will have your own interpretations, but there are certainly general meanings for each color that every one of us feels in common. We see rainbows and feel happy. We see dark clouds and feel sad. Spring green and yellow make us feel vibrant. You can even hear these meanings in everyday expressions describing each color: I feel blue when I am sad, red in the face when embarrassed, tickled pink when happy and green with envy when jealous! When doing readings, look at the different colors of the chosen crystals and have fun interpreting their meanings.

Color	Meaning	Interpretation
Red	Energetic, survival, physical, self preservation	Red represents the first chakra. It is grounding and physical. When red is present, I know that my client is able to move throughout life easily and is motivated. No red is a sign of a lack of physical movement. Too much red may indicate a need to take some time off and relax.
Black	**Grounded, stable, earthy, solid**	**Black is also a first chakra color. Black stones tell me my client is grounded. If they have too many black stones it tells me they may be materialistic and have a lot of worries or too much responsibility on their plate.**
Brown	**Earthy, practical, grounded**	**Brown is the third color associated with the first chakra. Brown stones tell me that my client enjoys being outdoors and is down-to-earth. However, if there are two or more brown stones, they might be weighed down with worry, as is the case with black stones.**
Orange	Enthusiasm, courage, self-confidence, social, passion, family oriented, nurturing, creativity	As a color of the second chakra, orange is always family oriented and feminine. No orange suggests a lack of home life, or not belonging. Too much orange could represent deep family problems, a need of support, or other relationship problems. If the stones have black in them, it may be a sign of sexual issues or abuse.

Peach	Wisdom, gentle strength, joy	Peach is another second-chakra color. It is very healthy and vibrant. It is a social color, telling me that my clients enjoy connecting with other people.
Yellow	Strength, intellect, happiness, motivated, self-empowered, social	Yellow is a sign of empowerment. The presence of yellow indicates the ability to stand up for oneself. Too many stones in this area is a sign of trying to assert power over another when it is not welcome. When there are no yellow stones it says to me that they feel powerless.
Green	Healing, peace serenity, harmony, compassion	The color of the fourth chakra is green, and when present, indicates an active heart, and the ability to feel. Multiple green stones mean they may have the ability to heal others. No green is a major problem. It indicates that the heart chakra is blocked. Green indicates masculine energy in a reading.
Magenta	Childhood stone, lack of family love, I need love	The magenta stones are also heart-chakra stones, but carry a child-like quality. I call my dark pink stones the "childhood issues" stone. A man or woman could pick this stone and it says to me "I need healing in the heart center from my childhood. My heart still hurts. Notice me!"
Pink	Self love, kindness, affection, heart felt love	Pink is a female-oriented heart chakra color. When someone chooses these stones, I know they are working on self- love. If I see a lot of pink their hearts may be too open, making them sacrificial. You may encounter readings, which will lack pink stones. This is fine if green is present.
Yellow Green	Cowardice, deceit, dishonest	When I see this stone in the heart chakra it means lack of courage and powerlessness. This green especially signifies a male. Take notice of the 5th and 3rd chakra they will indicate where the powerlessness originated.
Dark Green	Maturity, wisdom, patience, healing	This green heart chakra stone, when chosen, can indicate a strong calling to be a healer. It is the "green thumb" stone and most gardeners choose it. If more than one is chosen I would prescribe getting outdoors.
Light Green	Sympathy instead of empathy, immaturity, emotion healing	This heart-chakra color represents an immature ability to heal others. It is a high heart color and it signifies to me that some work is needed in that area. To achieve healer status I would encourage them to heal themselves first.

Blue Green	Spiritual, healer, trustworthy, helpful, loyal	This color is the fourth and fifth chakra. I rarely see this color chosen. I have one stone this color and it has never been chosen. Find a stone this color and interpret the meaning for yourself.
Turquoise	Communication and self expression	This is a fifth chakra color that when present says "I am creative." Too many says "I have something to say." No stones signify a lack of expression and an art form is needed.
Blue	Contentment, communicative, creative, devoted, self expression	This is a fifth chakra color. When I see lots of blue stones I feel that the person is creative, but not using their gifts. They have something very important to say. No blue? I would recommend a journal or taking art classes.
Indigo	Intuitive, spiritual, healing, wisdom, teacher	Indigo is the sixth chakra. When present, I feel that they may be very spiritual and have a good intuition. Lack of indigo means one needs to dream again. Too many stones means they have a lot on their mind… they're in the clouds!
Purple	Devotion, dignity, imagination, knowledge, spiritual	This third eye color says "I am spiritual and I have an imagination." When there is too much purple I feel that the person might be avoiding life and dreaming too much. If I see no purple I would ask them to try and remember their dreams.
White	Purity, perfection, oneness with God, connected, spiritual	White is connected with the crown chakra. When I see white, I feel that the person is connected to the universe. No white, I would ask them to connect to the universe by asking for what they want (Prayers).
Gold	Power, strength	When I see gold in a reading, I know it relates to the power chakra. Too many stones could mean they are overly materialistic and no gold is fine if yellow is present.
Gray	Fear, worries, depression	This color can be associated with either the crown chakra or the root chakra. I hold it aside and see it more as a heaven and earth stone. Torn between the two…

Bright colors- positive in nature, pure, clear
Pastels- immaturity, weak
Dark or muddy- negative qualities, fear, hate, anger, and greed

Crystals

Every crystal tells a different story: how I obtained it, the circumstances of my life at that time, and who or what it reminds me of. The energy of each story lingers with its crystal, and reveals something about the person who chooses it. I have a worry stone given to me by a friend when I was going through hard times, and a stone from Hawaii which both scream: "I need a vacation from my worries!" I have seen clients on many occasions with survival issues such as not having enough time or money, pick both crystals at the same time. Their prescription is to stop their day-to-day for a short period of time, taking one step back to move two steps forward. Relaxing always allows you to have clarity when making decisions, making better use of your time.

It is helpful to take note of feelings and thoughts surrounding the choosing of each of your crystals. They all have specific healing properties but they will also have their own sentimental meanings that will be tied to you and your readings. These insights will add to the meaning of each of them, and therefore give your readings more depth. When shopping for your crystals, write down the meanings and what personal thoughts went into the choice of each crystal. What were you thinking the day you picked it? Were you happy, hurried or totally relaxed? If someone gives you a stone, remember their age and what they may have been going through at that time. I have a pink rose quartz given to me by my son on Valentines Day, the perfect heart chakra stone on a heart-filled day. The crystal represents not only self-love, but also love given by another. When participants chose these stones, I know that their heart is full of love for themselves and that others love them. A client also gave me a small magenta heart-shaped stone on Valentine's Day. When someone draws this stone, I feel that they are in for some challenging times in the year ahead, specifically with loved ones. I have another stone that is dark orange, perfectly round and healthy. It has been repeatedly chosen by a client who was pregnant. She now has a healthy little boy. It is my, "Are you pregnant?" stone, and it has been right many times! These are a few my favorite crystals I've received as gifts, one comes from as far as London, England.

I have crystals that have been given to me and they all have specific meanings.
Can you match the meaning to the crystal?

1. A pointed yellow citrine given to me by my friend who was working on asserting herself with a man in her life. He told her she couldn't purchase it. She bought it anyway and used his money to buy it! I call it my pointed breast, "you can't tell me what to do" stone.

2. A large ocean-blue dolphin fin-shaped stone was given to me by a woman who accomplished her life's dream of swimming with the dolphins in Hawaii. I call it my "I need a spiritual vacation just for myself" stone.

3. A round blue stone, which looks healthy on one side, bu reveals a large black spot when turned over. This stone was given to my friend from his wife. He didn't want it and gave it to me. I call it my "lack of communication" stone.

4. A bright salmon colored stone with black veins running through it, given to me by a friend who went to New Orleans a year before Hurricane Katrina. At the time, he had high blood pressure with no logical explanation. I call it the "letting go of dammed up emotions" stone.

5. A perfect green malachite stone was chosen by the same friend on a very perfect synchronistic day, one year after the flood in New Orleans. I call it the "you can heal your heart" stone. Let it go and let it flow.

6. A large brown and grey striped worry stone given to me by a woman with whom I worked years ago, when I was going through my divorce. This stone has a long history, and when chosen, I know things are really bad and spiritual CPR is needed *stat*!

"You're black and beautiful, yellow, tan
you're white as light and soft as sand
with greens and greys and oh for days
a silver lining on the way..."
–Train *Your Every Color*

Gathering a Collection of Crystals

When choosing the number of crystals to pick from, it is best to start with a small amount. I suggest three healthy stones for each chakra as a starting point. Since we want to cover a range of states for each chakra (open, damaged, etc.), I would choose a healthy medium-sized stone first and then, a striped or black embossed stone and a large stone to represent each of the chakras. Healthy, unhealthy and too open is a good set of representations of the possible conditions. You do not need a special type of each crystal to verify blockages. When no stone is chosen, then that chakra is revealed to be closed. It is the lack of the crystal that verifies chakra blockages.

*Make certain that the chakras are equally represented in your collection of crystals. If you have too many of a given chakra, then your participants will be more likely to choose those stones.

Being able to recognize clear healthy stones from those that have imperfections will be very important in your readings, and in the growth of your crystal collection. Notice the difference between the two sets of stones pictured above. The appealing clear stones to the left represent healthy chakras. If you see any stones chosen in a reading from the second set, they will indicate *dis-ease* in that chakra. A starter set will contain a group of healthy stones. Slowly add those with imperfections, especially as you get better at identifying their meanings. The following stones are inexpensive and easy to find. I recommend them to start with:

- 7th chakra: Clear quartz crystal, moonstone and white snow quartz.
- 6th chakra: Amethyst, lapis lazuli and sodalite.
- 5th chakra: Turquoise, aquamarine and blue obsidian.
- 4th chakra: Rose quartz, malachite and jade.
- 3rd chakra: Tiger's eye, citrine and gold pyrite.
- 2nd chakra: Amber, orange carnelian and orange calcite.
- 1st chakra: Red jasper, obsidian and smoky quartz.

My crystals started in my car's ashtray and then were moved to a wooden box in my house. I now have them on a table in a large glass bowl. Most of my clients carry their crystals in a small cloth bag. After readings, I always give out a chakra prescription and a crystal to take home.

I now use over one hundred stones collected during the ten years that I have been doing readings. Each stone I use is unique, and they all feel like old friends of mine. I have oversized stones, small stones, sharp, and round stones. Some are lighter and some darker, and others are spotted black or ringed with white. All of these characteristics mean something specific to me. To really get to know the crystals, it is helpful to carry a crystal book with you and write down their meanings as you buy them.

Example: The Crystals and Characteristics

Amber: lifts your spirits, develops trust and promotes altruism
Amethyst: aids intuition, dreaming and imagination
Aquamarine: calms the nerves, promotes self expression and increases sensitivity
Carnelian: inspires courage, creativity and motivation
Citrine: enhances self esteem, confidence and mental clarity
Clear quartz: amplifies spirituality, connection and meditation
Hematite: aids in self-discipline, grounding and protection
Jade: balances the emotions, attracts prosperity and promotes clarity
Lapis lazuli: strengthens will, creativity and expression of emotions
Malachite: absorbs negative energy, heals the heart and encourages expressing feelings
Moonstone: promotes intuition, empathy and lucid dreaming
Obsidian: aids in protection, grounding and balance
Red Jasper: helps protect, strengthen and detoxify the body
Rose quartz: heals emotional wounds, restores love of self and heals the heart
Smokey quartz: relieves fear, lifts depression and grounds spiritual energy
Tigers eye: enhances confidence, self-esteem and mood lifting
Turquoise: aids self expression, creativity and communication with others

Connecting the Crystals, Colors, and Chakras

Knowing the colors of the stones and the associated chakras are the most important concepts when first learning to do readings. Here are a few examples:

Chakra	Color	Corresponding Stones
Seventh	White, Clear	Clear quartz crystal, moonstone, snow quartz, alexandrite
Sixth	Purple, Indigo	Purple sapphire, amethyst, sodalite, tourmaline, lapis lazuli
Fifth	Blue, Turquoise	Turquoise, blue topaz, aquamarine, sodalite, azurite, kyanite
Fourth	Green, Pink	Malachite, rose quartz, kunzite, emerald, green jade, green calcite, opal, aventurine, pink and green tourmaline
Third	Yellow, Gold	Citrine, tiger's eye, gold calcite, yellow jasper, pyrite
Second	Orange, Peach	Carnelian, amber, topaz, peach aventurine, orange calcite
First	Red, Black	Garnet, black tourmaline, obsidian, red jasper, smoky quartz

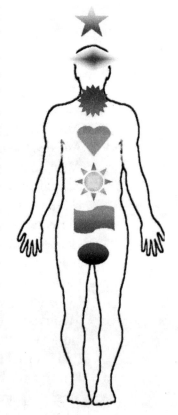

In my readings, I look for the amount of stones or size of stones chosen in the specific chakras. If, for instance, I see three amethyst stones then I know that the person who chose them is very imaginative and lives in their head. As you may guess, this means that the sixth chakra is too open, and would need to be closed slightly. If I saw no stones then I would have them open up that chakra by using their imagination and daydream a little throughout the day. Only one stone in the chakra suggests balance, as long as the stone was smooth and of a medium size. In most readings, you will see huge gaps, and the problem will appear obvious. If all of my client's stones lay above their heart chakra, I know that they must have their head in the clouds. On the other hand, a reading with all stones below the heart chakra is indicative of a person who is grounded, fears change, and has little imagination. Heart issues are the most common chakra blockages due to unresolved issues from childhood. A reading showing three or more "heart" stones, and none in the throat chakra, reveal that they need to get something off their chest, such as talking about a heart-related sadness from their past. Talking to someone who understands helps to reopen the heart chakra. Too many citrine or tiger's eye stones suggest that they have stomach problems and control issues, no stones in this area could represent a feeling of powerlessness in a relationship. This would lead me to look at the color of the heart stones to see if this feeling is associated with a man or a woman.

Heart Stones

Stones which indicate issues in the heart chakra can be inspected carefully for more clues, such as who the heart-related trouble is associated with. Rose quartz stones suggest it is a female and malachite, or green jade, hint at a male. This technique is a little advanced and it isn't always important to know the gender of the person associated with the pain. If I see more than two tainted green stones, I would ask what my client had to say about their father. If I see power issues related to the third chakra and a lot of pink or magenta stones (or "heart" chakra stones), the problem could be a mother-related issue from childhood. I have had a few readings which indicated that both a male and a female (tainted pink and green stones) were associated with the participant's heart chakra issues. The prescription is often to write a letter to each parent individually, expressing anything the participant may have wanted to say as a child. The letters are always private and for my client's eyes only! After the session, the letters are put to flame and released.

"Forgiveness means letting go of the past."–Gerald Jamposk

Most children tend to have no crystals representing their throat (5th chakra) and more than a few crystals representing their heart (4th chakra). When asked, they may have chronic sore throats and stomach aches (3rd chakra). Such an imbalance usually relates to a fear of expressing himself or herself in front of an intimidating parent, which pushes energy below the throat chakra. These children can often "feel" too much, and become oversensitive, tending to hold back tears. If they keep their thoughts to themselves (7th chakra), these thoughts may be expressed anyway while they sleep… as nightmares (6th chakra). Clearing up energy, removing blockages and opening closed chakras can allow energy to flow more freely throughout the body.

When seventh chakra crystals like moonstone and clear quartz are missing in the reading, I ask the participant to write down five things they would ask the universe for, if they could have anything they wanted. They may ask for the job of their dreams, a new home or a vacation. Let them brainstorm. Most clients will look down at the floor and say, "I just don't know, no one has ever asked me that question." When they look up, you will know they have succeeded in jumpstarting their seventh chakra. When they are done, they will have sent out their intentions into the world (prayers), eventually taking them from the ether of the spiritual world, working through their blocks, and finally manifesting them into physical form. Voila! Allowing one's imagination to run wild could be the key to making someone's dreams come true.

How to Start Your Readings

Let's now discuss the actual process of performing a crystal reading. To begin the reading, I clear my mind of all my daily chatter. I ask my Angels and guides to use me as an instrument and give me the courage to say out loud what they whisper into my mind, without hesitation. The person I am reading sits directly across from me, at a table; I find this is the best arrangement for me to use my intuition. I like one-on-one readings to be in a quiet room alone. That way, I only pick up the signals of the person in front of me. In relationship readings, it is important to have only the two people involved in the room; I find that people are much more relaxed and honest when others are not listening!

I always have a pen and paper with me and use it to write down their name and birthday before we begin, so I know their sign and their year number. I won't describe the significance of this information, or how to work with it, until later in this book. However, I'll give you a brief overview for the sake of describing the process of a reading. I discuss their sun sign and tell them what element it represents, such as air, earth, fire, and water. I also discuss their year cycle. For example, consider a client's birth date of March 30 and the year is 2005. Their sun sign is Aries and the year number is 3/30/2005, or 3+3+0+2+0+0+5=13, 1+3=4. Their year cycle number is four.

Our astrological knowledge suggests that this Aries individual may have a fiery personality and that leadership is important. Aries are passionate, aggressive and impulsive. The fourth year is a year to work hard in order to reap the benefits later. If I was reading an Aries in a fourth year I would tell them it is very important to finish the projects that they have already started. I will ask them what they started four years ago or if something dramatic happened at that time in their lives. Sometimes it is a new job, a new house or relationship. Whatever it is, they are in the year of truly taking time to nurture their new beginnings.

Understanding astrological traits and numerological phases helps tremendously in Relationship Readings. In our Aries example, if their companion is a water sign, we know who has the upper hand. Water can definitely put out fire's headfirst nature, which could be an advantage or disadvantage depending how the two work together. I would advise the Aries to stay on task and to ask the water sign to help put out any misdirected energy. Write down any information that might be helpful and move on to the choosing of the crystals.

A Reading with a Pisces born 2/22/88

In my readings, seven stones are drawn from a large glass bowl. I lay each stone they picked out on the table, starting with the white crown charka and ending with the red base, grouping the stones based on their colors (use the **Chakra Cheat Sheet** to practice). I then look at the stones they have chosen and discuss them. Which stones look healthy, which stones are oversized, which stones are light colored, or have black running through them? I discuss their meaning with the participant. Then, I move on to discussing the stones that are missing (the chakras that are not represented) and talk about what blockages they may have. You will have to refer to the chakras, colors and mind/body sections of this book until you are confident enough to read the stones from memory.

The Perfect Layout

The most important thing is to practice and to remember to use your intuition to guide you. The stones reveal blockages - what needs to be opened and what needs to be balanced to maintain spiritual health. I rarely see anyone with all seven colors. In fact, in all the years I have been doing readings, I have only seen two perfect layouts. Normally they are strong in some areas but are missing stones in others. They can be too "into" their head, or so grounded that they cease to daydream.

Health Issues and The Chakras

When the reading seems to be making progress, I will go a step further and turn my attention to health-related issues. If I see too many stones in one chakra, it may be an indication of illness. For example, three stones representing the sixth chakra may be indicative of migraines or headaches. If they have too many stones below the heart, I would ask about ulcers or stomach issues. The second chakra is associated with sexuality and family. When more than one stone is present it may indicate reproductive disorders or *dis-ease* in that area. Your intuition can do the detective work for you. Listen wholeheartedly and you might stumble onto something that could make some positive changes in the person you are reading. I continually get the, "I have never told anyone this before" phrase. That's the point at which I know I have hit on something important and that is why they need a reading. Everyone has something they would love to get off their chest or mind, if only someone would ask the right questions.

Astrology, numerology and most of the mind/body connection are advanced techniques and can be skipped until you perfect your knowledge of the chakras, colors and crystals. All other elements are "extras" in the readings. When you feel comfortable, add the choosing of the tarot and Angel cards first. Next, feel free to incorporate whatever comes natural to you. Remember, slow and steady always wins the race!

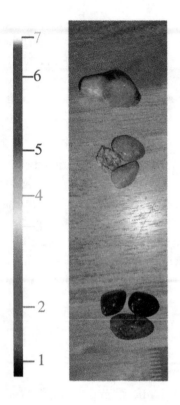

I had a reading with a woman who had three stones in her second chakra and they all had black running through them. She had too many throat stones: two of them were turquoise and the other was dyed blue. She also wore a turquoise colored sweater and earrings to match, so I knew she needed to say something. The oversized amethysts said to me that something huge was weighing on her mind. I asked a question about her family life (2nd chakra), and if she was having female issues which needed to be talked about. She replied "no," so I had her draw a tarot card. It was the nurturing mother card. Suddenly, she blurted out that she wanted to have a baby at 46. She informed me that she needed a hysterectomy due to tumors in her uterus and was pondering the fact that she would never have children. I asked her to write five reasons for having a baby. Her main reason was to bring her and her husband closer together. Looking at the list it was obvious that she wanted a child for all the wrong reasons. She later went ahead with the operation, having decided that having children was neither in her best interest nor in her husband's.

The blockages I see in the chakras cause *dis-ease* in the body. Headaches, sore throats and back pain can be a direct result of kinks in our chakra hoses. I had a man that wanted to stop chewing tobacco and had terrible neck and back pain, making it unbearable to go to work. He liked his job but was having to work only part time, not good for his spirit or wallet. His crystals showed no stones above his heart chakra. His throat chakra was the problem and the mind/body connection confirmed it. We related his chewing to his learning, in childhood, to keep his mouth shut due to the harsh words of his father. His heart stones were green and laced with black. His love for his father had backed up in his heart chakra and, like a blocked hose, was building up around his neck and jaw. His heart chakra was so large his chest looked oversized in proportion to the rest of his body. His closed throat chakra was his kink in his energetic hose and it was accumulating in his chest. He needed to express his heartfelt issues to open his throat area again. With such a build-up of energy, he could no longer afford to keep his mouth shut. His prescription was to write letters to his father, expressing all the words he needed to say when he was a child and had stored in his heart. He got the problem off his chest and felt better. He never gave the letters to his father but let them go by burning them. A fiery transmutation could have also helped resolve any anger issues stored in his third power chakra.

"Spiteful words can hurt your feelings but silence breaks your heart."-Unknown

This is how my readings progress, but remember all the rules can get thrown out the window if your intuition chooses a different path. I suggest that beginners skip steps 1-3 and step 7 until they have gained enough experience and feel comfortable with Crystal Readings.

1. Record the participant's name and birthdate
2. Explain sun sign and element
3. Explain life number and year
4. Choose seven crystals
5. Talk about the crystals chosen
6. Discuss blockages (crystals missing or too many in one chakra)
7. Ask mind/body questions
8. Pull tarot card and read out loud (three cards per reading)
9. Write down chakra prescriptions, up to three per reading (homework)
10. Finish with an Angel card
11. Choose a crystal to bring home

"The only real valuable thing is intuition."-Albert Einstein

Expanding Your Readings: Astrological Signs

Taking time to learn about the astrological signs gives you a great deal of important information. Before the participant even draws their stones, you can determine many important characteristics through understanding their sun sign and element. Understanding that someone's sun sign is a water sign, and therefore they have a tendency to be very emotional, may answer a lot of questions before their crystals are drawn. If you hate change, the celestial cause and effect are very obvious if it turns out that you are an earth sign.

Each sign is valuable and has its role. If I wanted to run a successful business, I would hire a Virgo to organize, an Aries to begin projects, a Gemini to do the advertising and a Cancer to nurture the project to completion. We can expand this concept to interpersonal relationships. Who does the talking in a relationship? Who seems in control? The signs could give you all the information you need. In any Relationship Reading, take the time to explain any differences between two or more signs. This helps your participants to understand themselves, and their loved ones, in a more enlightened way. For instance, if your parents were both water signs and you were a fire sign, you probably can identify with experiences where you were repeatedly "extinguished", but now you can see how this dynamic materialized. Understanding is the key to great relationships.

The Sun Signs are most important when doing Relationship Readings. Take the time to look up their element fire, earth, water or air and their sign's predominant nature. Explain to them their assets and what they may be learning from each other's differences. Remember to always be positive and look at what they have to offer one another.

Element Descriptions

Earth signs- Dependable, earthy, materialistic, sensual, patient, slow moving, consistent and grounded

Air signs- Freedom loving, optimistic, forgiving, changeable, detached, thoughtful, logical and analytical

Fire signs- Energetic, powerful, passionate, volatile, unstable, unpredictable, exciting and explosive

Water signs- Emotional, empathetic, serious, moody, deep, involved, stagnant and sensitive

Some signs can tolerate others for only a short time. These interactions could include friends, bosses and neighbors, yet valuable lessons can be learned if such impatience can be overcome. This insight is especially important if the opposing sign is someone with whom you *must* maintain harmony, such as your spouse, parent, child, or sibling.

I feel that we unconsciously bring certain types of people into our lives, so that we can learn certain lessons. What are the people in your life teaching you? Appreciating your differences could keep your relationships going smoothly by understanding each individual's strengths and vulnerabilities. Recognizing these characteristics is the most important thing you can do to maintain a long-lasting love for someone you normally would never talk to!

I have three children: one is an Aries, another is a Gemini, and my son is a Taurus. They are like night, day and late afternoon. As a parent, I thought if I get the first one trained – the same techniques will work on the others… Nope! It doesn't work that way. When the headstrong Aries had disciplinary trouble in school, the teachers would call home and I would say the same thing: "Don't tell her 'sit down!' ask her 'would you like to take your seat?' " They would call back and say "thank you!" How many teachers do children have in a lifetime? With my Aries daughter, I believe I spoke to them all, including a few of her school's principals. My airy Gemini was very wispy and social. Unlike my Aries and Taurus, the Gemini didn't play sports, but waited until high school to be a cheerleader. A prototypical Gemini, she jumped at any opportunity to use her voice and be social. My earthy Taurus is rock-hard, solid, slow and methodical. "Hurry up!" was our constant mantra when he was small. He is the bull: slow to anger but watch out if you fly red in front of him. Not all signs are consistent, but knowing the signs can be quite helpful when planning with whom you want to spend time! If I want to "crowd surf" at a concert I will take my Aries daughter. She will be the first to throw me into the air. If I want to go sing Karaoke I will take my Gemini, and she will sing over my untrained voice. If I want to stay home, cuddle and watch a movie, I will hang out with my Taurus son.

The Sun Signs and Their Elements

Fire Signs (Inspirational)- Aries, Leo, Sagittarius
Earth Signs (Practical)- Taurus, Virgo, Capricorn
Air Signs (Mental) - Gemini, Libra, Aquarius
Water Signs (Emotional)- Cancer, Scorpio, Pisces

Elemental Pairings

Air and Air- Mentally, emotionally and spiritually uplifting. Air can become stagnant, too comfortable and stale. Freedom is very important to fan the wind of change for these two.

Fire and Fire- Passionate hot flames can consume themselves or light up the darkness, watch for burnout. Time alone can be critical for this pair to avoid a supernova.

Earth and Earth- This relationship is stable, strong and dependable. Like can attract like. Earthy sensuality could turn into boredom. Keep things moving and remember that change can be uplifting.

Water and Water- Emotionally compatible if kept flowing together, watch out for the dams of blocked emotions that can cause stagnation and buildup. Open communication about how they feel is very important with this pair.

Fire and Air- Air feeds fire, passionate yet combustible… too much time together could create explosive situations. Outside interests are very important for these two elements to create warm embers together.

Fire and Earth- Contradicting, earth (dirt) puts out fire and fire heats up earth (wood). Balance and total respect for one another is the only way these two can last without consuming each other.

Fire and Water- Water puts out fire. These opposites could destroy each other, and yet opposites do attract. Understanding each other's strengths and differences is the only way these two can heat things up and create a steamy relationship.

Earth and Air- Earth can smother air, air loves freedom and earth loves staying in one place. Tolerance and understanding with a lot of patience could keep these two together for a while, but be wary of this eventually turning into sacrifice on both ends.

Earth and Water- This could be too emotionally restrictive for water signs. Earth can stop the emotional flow of water. With calculated emotional release, this pair can make the dessert green and lush, or otherwise make a mudslide!

Air and Water- Air and water do not mix; air and water make for emotionally stormy weather. Air becomes heavy and weighed down, forming clouds and then rain. Tolerance and respect for a non-controlling relationship can work.

"Consider how hard it is to change yourself and you will understand how little chance you'll have in trying to change others." –Unknown

The Infant and the Elder

The signs exist in a sequence relating to maturity and age. This timeline begins with Aries, an infant sign, and ends with Pisces, the elder sign. Aries is impulsive and Pisces wise and slow. Knowing this timeline is an asset, giving you another piece of information to help you assemble your participant's astrological personality profile. If I am a Capricorn, and married to an Aries, who will try and lead? Who would win out in a relationship between the old man Capricorn and the infant Aries? More often than not, the headstrong Aries will wear out the Capricorn over time, as the old man would tire of the impetuous infant. Keep in mind all of the sun signs' positions on this timeline when doing Relationship Readings.

The Cusps

A person is said to be a "cusp" when they are born on a day during the sun's transition from one sign to the next. The tension within an individual born on a cusp can produce a single reading that resonates with an air of a Relationship Reading, because there are two signs attempting to exist harmoniously within one person. You can let these individuals know that they have two distinct people inside of them. For example, if the participant is on a cusp between an earth and an air sign (i.e. Capricorn/Aquarius), they may love freedom and want to be the social butterfly, yet do not want to leave the house. They could have some fighting going on between their two selves: one who loves change and the other who is afraid to try new things. Their differences, when viewed constructively, may be an asset because they help to achieve balance in life. If I am a Taurus and forced to move a lot because of my job or family, I will always feel unhappy because a Taurus needs a stable family life to flourish. A Taurus will often fight change, but a Gemini on the other hand, would love a changing environment. A Taurus/Gemini cusp may strike a balance, like having a job that allowed one to travel occasionally.

A Leo/Cancer cusp is another tough one, fire and water, powerful yet emotional. Their powerful emotions may be too much for most people to handle. People on this cusp may find themselves alone quite often. They are hard to be around, and very difficult to live with. Finding an outside activity to allow them to blow off emotional steam would help in maintaining relationships.

Sagittarius/Capricorn cusps are also difficult: stable yet unpredictable. Earth with fire is conflicting, and the struggle between these signs can swing someone back and forth in so many directions that they can feel paralyzed with ambivalence. Knowing this would remind you not to beat yourself up for taking so long to make decisions in your life. Being understanding with yourself helps ease the stress associated with taking the necessary steps to your next destination.

A Libra/ Scorpio cusp could be the most opposing combination, water and air. If you look at the element connection, they don't mix well. Yet, if you combine the two sun signs you find an intense, emotional person who has difficulties weighing out the decisions to be made in their lives. They may be too deep for most people to deal with on a daily basis. They would make great stage actors if they could decide what role they wanted to play. Their best relationships could be found in groups that fight for justice and have a cause in common, working for Green Peace comes to mind.

Cardinal, Fixed, and Mutable

Cardinal- (Leaders, pioneers, inventors) Aries, Cancer, Libra, Capricorn
Fixed- (Organizers, arranger, processor) Taurus, Leo, Scorpio, Aquarius
Mutable- (Communicator, conveyor, informer) Gemini, Virgo, Sagittarius, Pisces

Opposing Characteristics

Masculine- (Direct and energetic) Aries, Gemini, Leo, Libra, Sagittarius, Aquarius
Feminine- (Receptive and magnetic) Taurus, Cancer, Virgo, Scorpio, Capricorn, Pisces

The Sun Signs

(Sun sign dates from www.stariq.com)

Aries
The Ram ("I AM")
March 20- April 19

[handwritten: CARDINAL]

Health: Head, face, eyes, nose, ears
Positive: Brave, active, passionate, determined, intellectual, competitive
Negative: Combative, impulsive, insensitive, self-centered, forward, aggressive

Taurus

[handwritten: Fixed]

The Bull ("I HAVE")
April 20-May 20
Health: Throat, neck, glandular system
Positive: Affectionate, stable, patient, loving, loyal, earthy
Negative: Lazy, materialistic, stubborn, possessive, resistant to change, cheap

Gemini
The Twins ("I COMMUNICATE")
May 21- June 20

[handwritten: MUTABLE]

Health: Arms, hands, shoulder, nervous system, lungs
Positive: Expressive, intellectual, logical, thoughtful, clever, energetic
Negative: Indecisive, superficial, restless, fickle, nervous, analytical

Cancer
The Crab ("I FEEL")
June 21-July 22

[handwritten: CARDINAL]

Health: Breast, chest, stomach
Positive: Nurturing, warm, loyal, devoted, wise, sentimental
Negative: Possessive, moody, supersensitive, defensive, withdrawn, obstinate

Leo
The Lion ("I CREATE")
July 23- August 22

[handwritten: FIXED]

Health: Back, heart, spine
Positive: Sensual, funny, warm, generous, courageous, self-confident
Negative: Possessive, selfish, intimidating, immature, unfaithful, lazy, prideful

Virgo
The Virgin ("I SERVE")
August 23- September 22
Health: Intestines, spleen, stomach   *MUTABLE*
Positive: Orderly, honest, dependable, loyal, practical, hardworking
Negative: Worrier, particular, perfectionist, workaholic, critical, shrewd

Libra
The Scales ("I WEIGH")
September 23-October 22
Health: Kidneys, abdomen, pancreas   *CARDINAL*
Positive: Warm hearted, diplomatic, balanced, active, calm, harmonious
Negative: Paralyzed, over-rational, detached, stoic, intolerant, aloof

Scorpio
FIXED The Scorpion ("I CONTROL")
October 23- November 21
Health: Groin, genitals, reproductive system, colon
Positive: Passionate, sexual, powerful, intuitive, emotional, sensitive
Negative: Vengeful, secretive, controlling, jealous, stubborn, unforgiving

Sagittarius
The Archer ("I PHILOSIPHY")
November 22-December 21
Health: Hips, thighs, liver, gall bladder   *MUTABLE*
Positive: Energetic, freedom-loving, fun, spontaneous, charismatic, outgoing
Negative: Impulsive, unstable, scattered, outspoken, rude, unloving

Capricorn
The Goat ("I MASTER")
December 22- January 19
Health: Knees, bones, teeth   *CARDINAL*
Positive: Reserved, incisive, highly ambitious, practical, realistic, mature
Negative: Materialistic, gloomy, negative, boring, frugal, rigid

Aquarius
The Water Bearer ("I UNIVERSALIZE")
FIXED **January 20- February 18**
Health: Legs, ankles, shins
Positive: Helpful, intellectual, independent, assertive, sincere, social
Negative: Cold, detached, opinionated, eccentric, erratic, fanatical

Pisces

The Fish ("I BELIEVE")

February 19-March-19

Health: Feet, toes, lymphatic system, circulation
Positive: Receptive, intuitive, gentle, imaginative, sensitive, spiritual
Negative: Shy, self destructive, passive, addictive, idle, ineffective

Positive and Negative

Like the chakras, sun signs each exhibit unique negative and positive characteristics when in and out of balance. For instance, Pisces are wise healers when healthy, but when unbalanced, they may be addictive and detached. A grounded Sagittarius is fun, but too much freedom makes them impulsive. We are here to learn from one another via our relationships. Thank god for our differences and the lessons they teach us.

I am a Gemini that can't sit still and wholeheartedly embraces change. I love that my Taurus, Virgo and Capricorn friends and family are so dependable. I also enjoy the passion of the fire signs in my life. As an air sign, I prefer fire signs only because of their heat, as long as I know when enough is enough and have the willpower to pull away. Sometimes I simply find a water sign to cool things down. Water signs are great listeners when you need to emote. If I want comfort, I seek out an air sign. There is a sign for every season.

"There is nothing either good or bad, but thinking makes it so."-William Shakespeare, *Hamlet*

Example: The Social Butterfly

I begin my readings by identifying the individual's sun sign and explaining its characteristics. During one particular reading, I told a young woman that she was an Aquarius (air sign, fixed and masculine) the social butterfly, independent and assertive. She said that my description didn't portray her at all. After a few more readings, I asked her if she would like to take one of my classes. She said, "I can't," and that she didn't like being around other people. At that time, she was experiencing significant powerlessness at home, a lack of ability to express herself, and chose to retreat into herself, to avoid any type of social interaction. In our first reading together, her prescription was to take charge of her surroundings by throwing away the stuff her mother had given her (Feng Shui) that she really didn't like (metaphoric). She struggled with the thought of challenging her mother's authority in her own home! The word "no" was not yet in her vocabulary. She later went home and was instantly amazed at how much "stuff" she had in her house that was not her own, but her mother's. What a revelation! The day of our second appointment, she was on her way when she called me in tears and said she couldn't come because her boyfriend wouldn't let her. I told her that it was her choice and that I would be waiting for her if she changed her mind. When I opened my office door she was sitting in the hall with a smile on her face. She found the courage to come for her reading and passed a huge power chakra test. I saw in many of her readings that she was losing her power to a man (pointed green/yellow stone) but I didn't need to point that out to her. She figured it out on her own. She continued to do her homework over many sessions, and after a year, she convinced her boyfriend to come in for a Relationship Reading on Valentine's Day. He was a Leo (fire sign, fixed and masculine) and seemed to wear the pants at home and their reading confirmed it. Their prescription that day was to make valentines for one another, encouraging them to re-open their heart chakras.

When I went into the next room to see how they were doing, he hadn't started his and had left. She started by saying, "I love you" in her card and then inside was a sad frown. He walked out without even making an effort. It was obvious he didn't want to change, but in the days to come, she did. After being her true self for months she decided that he might not be the man for her. So, of course, he bought a ring and asked her to marry him!?!? She said "no," and continued to do readings with me. More than a year later, we attended a meditation class together, forgetting that she didn't like to be around a lot of other people. During our class together she told the teacher, "Dena doesn't heal you, she gives you the tools to heal yourself!" After transforming herself, she has in fact become the social butterfly!

People in our lives will never change if we simply stay the same. When we take it upon ourselves to change, the people in our lives change with us accordingly, or simply fall away. In the end, we may suddenly open ourselves up to new relationships that fit the new way we feel about ourselves. The Aquarius and Leo are still figuring out who is the king or queen of the jungle! I am sure she chose him to learn about her strengths (he is, after all, a Leo) and I am sure he was attracted to her so he could eventually open up his heart (Valentines Day). If they stay together or split up, it may seem to make a difference in this world, but in the grand scheme of things, it is the lessons that they are learning from one another that really matter.

When doing relationship readings, be aware that certain signs are attracted to one another because their partner's qualities compensate for what they may be missing. For instance, if you have a married couple who fight because the wife is always spending money and the other is frugal, look to see if one is Taurus and the other Capricorn. The Taurus loves material luxuries and a Capricorn loves security. They both want the same thing and that is why they were drawn together, to have a beautiful and well-decorated stable home. They would need to achieve a common vision and start over again. If they can recapture this common vision and set some boundaries, they will continue on their stable journey. Since they are both earth signs they may need to shake things up a bit and invite a few fire signs over for dinner!

I did a reading for a couple - one an Aries and the other a Cancer. They were extreme opposites, fire and water. It seemed to me that the water could have had the upper hand by putting out the fiery will of the Aries, but the fire sign was overcompensating and evaporating the water as if it were in a pan over a hot flame. The water sign's heart was wide open and the fire sign was assertive and bullied the other. The big-hearted water sign always sat silently while the fire sign did all of the talking. For their prescription, I asked them to change roles. He was going to speak for ten minutes without interruption. She said he wouldn't be able to do it. I had him read something from a book out loud so he wouldn't run out of things to say. Not surprisingly, he started and paused for a single comma when she suddenly burst out saying "see, I told you he couldn't do it."

"Knowledge speaks, but wisdom listens" -Jimi Hendrix

In order to really understand the pairing of signs and their traits, let's consider an extreme example. We have two participants Crystal Reed and Rocky Game who are dating. She is a Pisces water sign, and he is a Leo fire sign. Pisces are feminine, receptive, and emotional, but they are also cardinal signs who like to be in charge. Leos are masculine, direct, and energetic, but they are a also fixed signs who don't like to be told what to do. I wouldn't want to be entirely negative, but these two have the makings of a disasterous romance.

Sun, Moon and Ascending Signs

There is way too much information related to astrology to cover in this book alone. This is just a brief description. Everyone has a sun, moon and an ascending sign. If I am a Gemini sun, Gemini moon and have a Gemini ascending, it would be pretty easy to predict that I love to communicate and socialize. If, for example, I am a Gemini sun, Cancer moon and Pisces ascending, I may love to talk but I could be overly mothering, ultra-sensitive and emotional. Notice the conflicting elements air and double water. When doing Crystal Readings, it isn't necessary to get so involved in astrology. However, as you educate yourself and deliver better readings, this information may benefit you. Getting your birth chart done can help you understand astrology and is a lot of fun.

Expanding Your Readings: Numerology

Just as astrology can provide a lot of insight into a person's personality, numerology can give you an understanding of what stage of life they are in, and what they are meant to achieve. When I begin a reading, I have the client write their full name and birth date. I then add up the numbers. For instance, if their birth date is January 1st, I will add the month's number to the day's number, or 1+1=2. I then add the 2 to the now current year. For instance, 2004 is 2+0+0+4=6. A six year, and a two birth date, add together to become eight, or 6+2=8.

In the above example, the person would be in an "eight" year. Life cycles go from one to nine. Each number has its own meaning in terms of the great cycle of life, death, and rebirth. In our example, this person would be almost at the end of a 9-year cycle. Whatever they planted 8 years ago has come to fruition, withered, and died. Was it a bountiful harvest? Now is the time to take inventory and plan for the future, while learning from the past. When we see a "one" year, it is the beginning - we get to replant.

The nine-year cycle is very important in readings. We may discover that we have closure, or we have to learn patience and wait for the harvest. If we have sowed our seeds and are reaping the harvest, we need to sit it out and think of what changes we need to make in the future. If we want to have a fruitful harvest, we must take care of our seedlings in the early years. If we are in the first part of planting, we must continue weeding out old ideas and nurturing the new. These can take the form of relationships that hold us back which we may have outgrown. In the latter part of our cycle, when our garden starts to die, we must have an idea of what we want in the next chapter of our lives. Taking great care of our thoughts and investing in our future are the most important things we can do at this late stage. Focusing on what we want to plant and leaving the past behind us gives us the seeds we need for new growth!

"The years teach much, which the days never knew."-Ralph Waldo Emerson

The Nine-Year Cycle Numbers

Number	Season	Descriptor	Interpretation
1	Late winter Early spring	Pioneer	New beginnings, it is time to break ground. The earth is in need of a turn, and we have begun to cultivate it. Thoughts are so important here because we are pondering what we want for new growth in our lives. We may be inspired to grow a new healthier garden or possibly plant the same crop from last year. We can be ripe for change or dead set on remaining the same.
2	Spring	Patience	Be cooperative and do not force anything, pay attention to detail. We have started the process, what does the ground look like? Full of weeds or old growth? If weeding is needed, we must start over and keep the ground fertile. Get rid of the old and prepare for the new. This could involve dissolving old relationships, leaving old jobs or deciding that it's time to move. Plant new seeds.
3	Late spring	Enjoyment	Believe in yourself, because seeds are beginning to send out roots. We have begun to plant and it is late spring. We have weeded out the old and planted our ideas. If we held on to some "weedy" relationships we will find that we may feel regretful and angry that we held onto negative people and/or past issues. This is a time for inner work and learning from our past.
4	Early summer	Practical	Attend to details, the more you give the more you get. We have begun to see what we have planted. Our ideas have sprouted and we must be vigilant to water, weed and keep the sun shining on our garden. If we did not choose to grow in the past, we will feel that our garden could be so much more and we will begin to ponder another crop. It is too late to turn back now.
5	Summer	Change	We are waiting for the harvest, and hopefully embracing what we have planted. We may see a satisfying harvest blooming, or we may feel disappointed with what we have chosen to plant. Now is the time to be thankful and to wholeheartedly keep tending to our garden. This is the year to accept our choices and to begin to visualize what we will do differently next time around.
6	Late summer	Responsibility	We may have regrets that we didn't work harder toward a greater vision. On the other hand, we may be drenched in satisfaction and bathing in the beauty that we have cultivated, finding ourselves on vacation. This is late summer and all we do is take in what we have done for the last 6 years. Going to town and seeing what others may have planted inspires us to achieve a healthier crop in the coming seasons.
7	Fall	Faith	Reflect, ponder and meditate. In fall, good weather allows our plants to still thrive. We are preparing for the end and reaping our harvest. Yet, thoughts of our next cycle are prevalent. This is the year to really put into writing what we have learned and where we would like to be headed. If the harvest is good, we are patting ourselves on the back and getting ready to rest.

8	Late Fall	Achievement	Take it to the market, and let it go. Taking in the last of the harvest can be satisfying or disappointing, depending on how earnest your efforts were. Were the crops scarce or abundant? Do we build on our current ways of thinking or start from scratch? We have a choice. What we do is in our power. We either bask in the bounty or prepare for famine. This year is desolate for those who are stuck in their old ways. Those who were prepared get to enjoy and relax.
9	Winter	Completion	This is not a time to start anything. Winter is all about endings and letting go. The plants die and we look at what we have accomplished and where we are going next. At winter's end, spring will soon be around the corner! Change is necessary no matter how abundant your life is, because you always have to be growing and learning. What have you to take with you into spring? What lessons have you learned and what wisdom will you take forward with you into our next life cycle?

* There are two other important year cycles to take note of. One is an 11/2, meaning a very intuitive year and you are to shine like a star. Set new standards for yourself, achieving inner growth and illumination. The other is a 22/4 year, signifying greatness and superior accomplishments. It is a master number. (*Colors and Numbers* by Louise Hay). Take June 9th for an example and the year 2005, 6+9+2+0+0+5=22, 2+2=4. This year is a 22/4. Working on big plans for the good of the many will be worthwhile and prosperous. I am writing this book in a 22/4 year!

To find the chosen life lesson of the participant you add all of the relevant numbers representing their birth date plus their birth year, instead of the current year, as in the case with determining the nine-year cycle number. For example, the birth date June 9, 1964: 6(month)+9(day)+1+9+6+4(year)= 35, 3+5=8. This person's life number is 35/8. Abundance and power are the intended themes of their life lesson. You can also take into consideration the three and five separately: expression and sensitivity, freedom and discipline.

The life numbers

1	Creativity and Confidence
2	Cooperation and Balance
3	Expression and Sensitivity
4	Stability and Process
5	Freedom and Discipline
6	Vision and Acceptance
7	Trust and Openness
8	Abundance and Power
9	Integrity and Wisdom
0	Inner Gifts

Inner Gifts and "Zero"

Occasionally, your participant's life number will have a zero. The zero is especially important because it relates to inner gifts, and emphasizes the leading number it is associated with. For example, someone who was born March 30, 1975 (3+3+0+1+9+7+5) = 28 = 10... The zero means "inner gifts" and places emphasis on creativity and condifence - the "1" (Adapted from Dan Millman's The *Life You Were Born to Live).*

Intuition and Guidance

Your intuition is the most important tool you will use in Crystal Readings, so have a pen and paper with you at all times to quickly write down the signals and messages that are "spoken" to you during the course of a reading. Write down any thoughts, visions, or single words that float through your mind. Your confidence in yourself is critical, and practice makes perfect! Second-guessing yourself will weaken your intuition and will harm your ability to truly see beyond a person's facade. Sometimes, the strangest thoughts can float through your head during the course of a reading. However, just because these thoughts seem odd to you doesn't mean that they are not meaningful when put in context. If your "inner voice" tells you to say something, just go for it. If you hear yourself say, "don't say that, they will think you're crazy," you'll find your intuition was actually right. Have the courage to say what you feel and it will turn out right in the end. Never second-guess yourself.

Again, words that seem irrelevant may have meaning, so write them down and say them out loud when appropriate. Taking an example from my own experience, I did a reading on a woman who came to me for help with depression. I repeatedly saw the words "black and white pictures." When I spoke about this to her, she shrugged and told me "I don't know what that means." As the reading went on, however, the crystals said she was lacking a creative outlet. Later, she said she had been pondering buying a camera so she could take pictures of her children, specifically black and white photos! Remember, the person you are reading might tell you that they have no idea what you are talking about. However, when the reading is over, it will all come together.

If various emotions arise during a reading, simply tell the participant what you are feeling. An intuitive will feel the emotional energy of the people around him or her. You may also get physical sensations within your body. Make note of them. You may hit upon something very important within their bodies. For instance, I have done readings for couples that I felt intuitively that they had been fighting before they arrived and they swore everything was fine. During the reading, they begin to feel more comfortable and the crystals will correlate with that same sensation. That is when they are ready to discuss the disagreement from a higher ground.

When used correctly, empathy is a gift. However, if you have a hard time differentiating your emotions from theirs, then it is best to not use this technique. If you do find yourself in this situation, just say, "I choose not to feel this right now" and it should stop. Also, protecting yourself with a bubble of white light and washing your hands between readings will help you shed the energy you pick up during your sessions. In order to maintain your intuitive state, you must take care of your body, your mind and your spirit. I often find that I am not grounded following readings and that food will keep me from feeling too airy. I also drink water during readings and eat something with protein before I begin. The lighter your diet, the easier it is to be in synch with the people you are reading. Exercise and a good night's sleep also help me deliver a better reading. When doing multiple readings, make sure you shower or take a long bath before you go to bed. Allowing any unwanted energy to go down the metaphoric drain.

Most of the readings I have given are fun and enlightening – focusing on the "lighter" side. Yet, there have been many times I have known that I've had help, where my guides stepped in and the reading was there to encourage my client to make some major life changes. If I said something astonishingly true, it isn't only me. It's also *them*. They call themselves *Light Beings*. I call *them* my voices or my Angels! You will know you are giving a great reading when the "coincidences" start to appear, I call them synchronicities. Sometimes, I simply sit back and let *them* drive. When this happens, I am just an instrument. The only thing I regret is not always being able to take notes because I have gotten some incredible spontaneous insights during my readings, many of them truly T-shirt worthy one-liners. If I am really **on**, I tend to start rhyming in my sessions. I will try and remember what I said so I can write it down but the words sometimes escape me. I believe the universe truly has a sense of humor.

You may not be able to relay your intuitions to the person with the correct language, but using your intuition will never mislead you. The person you're reading may not understand what you've said until that night, in their dreams, or while reading a book days later. Nevertheless, just be yourself and relay any insights and information as best as you can. Remember to be encouraging, never discouraging! I have had a few readings that I saw something I felt I couldn't share with the person at that time, but I knew that the appropriate time would be revealed later. One cannot underestimate the value of discernment. You are not doing readings to "fix" people but to guide and educate them about themselves.

I did a reading for a friend of mine right before Christmas. He pulled his stones and they told me he needed to open his throat chakra. I have always seen him as a writer (I call him my Jewish scribe from a past life), so we were pondering what he could write about. He pulled a card from the Tarot and he got the *hangman* card. I would normally ask "what are you hung up on at this time?" but my intuition took over and I asked what he thought the card meant to him. He said all he could think of was something that had taken place in the 9th grade. He told me a story about a young man he went to school with who he thought had accidentally taken his life. He explained that after watching a movie about an execution during the civil war, his friend thought that he could outsmart the hangman by slipping out of the noose. His friend was killed trying to do so alone one day in his home. Every one thought it was suicide, but my friend felt that it was an accident. I asked him if he had told anyone and he said "only you." I normally would have continued with the reading and have him pull two more cards but the prescription was obvious, he would write a letter to the parents and get this incident off his chest, opening his throat chakra. He didn't know if he could find their address, but I intuitively knew that he would. Every reading I do is personal and always different than the last, but this reading was guided by intuition to such a degree, that I felt that his friend had somehow spoken to us that day. It is the stuff that makes the hair on your arms stand straight up!

In the days to follow, my friend found the address, wrote the letter and sent it to the family. Sadly, that same week the second son had killed himself in the family's home in the same way that his brother had done so many years ago. The parents were incredibly distraught and were blaming themselves for the deaths of their two sons. The letter, proclaiming that their first son had indeed not taken his own life on purpose, was an incredible relief to the distraught parents at such a heart-wrenching time. They wanted to meet with my friend right away to thank him for his message. The synchronicities spiraled from there and came full circle back into his and his family's life. What are the odds?

Intuition isn't a gift, we all have it. Some use it, others don't. As you do your own readings, you will find that intuition is associated with the higher chakras, and clearing energy in these areas will open you up to your own feelings, inner voice, sight and knowing. I had a client who closed his third eye early in childhood because he learned how not to see what was taking place in his family's home. This had a collection of effects, the most pronounced of which was that he had lost his sense of smell and wore thick glasses, both associated with the sixth chakra. After a reading with me he returned to his own home while his wife was doing laundry. Amazingly, he couldn't help but comment on the smell of bleach, which filled the house. His wife said it always smelled that way when she washed the clothes. In our session, he had opened up his third eye, just by discussing what he didn't want to see when he was younger. In my practice, I use guided imagery and color therapy to help my clients open their third eye. Having a participant close their eyes, imagine a color and see themselves accomplishing their goals is another way to help jumpstart the sixth chakra. If that is not possible, then their chakra is blocked.

I believe eyesight is an indication of a strong intuition. I used to wear glasses when I was younger and now I don't. I have been told many times that I have great eyesight and those around me comment on how well I can see, just as they put on their eyeglasses. Though it may seem miraculous, I outgrew my glasses by forcing myself to see what was going on around me and face it head-on, rather than putting on blinders. If I see an adult wearing glasses, I know there is something going on that they refuse to see. Sure enough when asked, they started to lose their eyesight around a painful period in their life.

Well-tuned hearing is another sign of good intuition. A sensitive ear suggests that you have intuition, but are you listening to what your voice is saying? If you are in a group of people and your inner voice is going against the majority, how many times can you tell it to be quiet before you lose the ability to hear it? I remember a time when my voice was so faint I almost lost it. I wasn't being true to myself and therefore I was facing a spiritual death; it was a difficult time in my life. There were no synchronicities, and I always felt as if I was in the wrong place, banging my head up against someone else's wall. It is not a fulfilling way to live and is really quite painful. However, I am grateful to have gone through such an experience, because without it, I wouldn't know the difference. You must value your inner voice; only then can you act upon what is being whispered to you… every minute!

To take action on your intuitions, your lower chakras also have to be healthy. The courage to use your voice involves the lower chakras, which give you the confidence to act upon what your intuition tells you. I remember the day I opened up my eyes, looked around, and made some huge changes in my life, guess what… nobody liked it! If I didn't have the confidence to follow my voice, I might have wilted and become the person that everyone else wanted me to be. I know the difference between becoming one with my own voice, and casting that voice aside. Embracing my inner voice means that life is truly filled with joy and is playful. Listen to yourself, write down how you want to spend your days, and do one thing daily that is truly just for you, and for no one else. Be yourself, love yourself and listen to that small still voice every chance you get.

"For whereas the mind works in possibilities, the intuitions work in actualities, and what you intuitively desire, that is possible to you." -D H Lawrence

Expanding Your Readings: The Tarot

I have mentioned the use of various types of cards in describing some of my example readings. These cards are a way of adding a little more "divinity" to the reading. However, I feel it necessary to clarify my use of Tarot cards. Keep in mind, as I describe my methods, that I am not performing actual Tarot readings. I am only using a few of the cards to allow my guides to aid me and give me clues as to what my participant's concerns might be. For guidance on how to perform full Tarot readings, I suggest you pick up a book on that specific subject.

After I have interpreted and discussed the chosen crystals with my client, I shuffle the cards three times and then fan them out on the table. When I intuitively feel that the time is right, or when there is a break in discussion, I have them choose a card. We discuss it and then pick two more before the reading is finished. Tarot cards, Angel cards, and other types of divination media are all suitable, and everyone will develop their own preference. I prefer to have a set of Tarot or Angel cards. Interestingly, the card's theme is always relevant to what we have discussed in reading their crystals. I believe Angels (Light Beings) may whisper, "Pick that one", to my client… and tah dah! They almost always ask in amazement, "How do you do that?" I simply say, "I don't, you have the power to do it, and you do it for yourself with the help of your guides and Angels." I believe that this is an example of the universe speaking directly to us, aiding the soul in search of itself.

I once did a reading with a group of women starting their own business. Before I arrived, I saw a dark cloud and a rainbow over the establishment. When I started the reading, I shared what I saw with them. It seemed that day they had been served with papers from the last landlord and they might lose their lease. In the reading, each person drew a card relating to floods, rain and disaster – even one titled *Setback*! Yet, each card also revealed a rainbow! It wasn't easy, but the black cloud lifted and their business venture smoothly fell into place. They survived the incident and, again, the cards worked perfectly in the reading. I wished them luck in finding gold at the end of their rainbow.

Most sets of cards come packaged with a small booklet, explaining the meaning of each card. You may study the meanings to become more familiar with the world of Tarot. Memorizing these meanings allows you to discuss the cards with the participant with confidence. However, if they read the card's meaning from the book aloud, it keeps them involved. And by reciting the empowering and insightful words for themselves, instead of hearing me talk all the time, they feel energized and more empowered. I usually have people pick up to three cards, but there have been times that my inner voice told me to personally draw one card for them. I will set aside a card if they accidentally draw two, or one card is conspicuously sticking out of the spread. I had a reading with a woman whose stones indicated that she needed to clear some stagnant energy from her power chakra. She explained that she was mourning the death of her friend and hadn't completed the grieving process. What she really needed to do was emote and not feel that crying was a weakness. When I turned over the fourth card that I had put aside until the end of the reading, it was the *death* card. The death card represents endings, but also new beginnings and rebirth. I felt her friend's presence and her tears began to flow. The cards helped in a way that I could have never expressed in words. Letting go of your perceptions, being spontaneous and listening to your intuition is the key to a successful reading.

"We come to beginnings only at the end."-William Throsby Bridges

Synchronicities

I also tell people to look for synchronicities, such as books that open to the right pages, or TV shows or songs that say exactly what you need to hear - the coincidences that happen to help change your life. Paying attention to these signals can give you clues, helping you tell the difference between the right and wrong paths to take in life. I only move forward with major decisions in my life when synchronicities are abundant, usually coming in threes. If I don't get the green light to move ahead, I will sit it out and wait. This could mean stopping to meditate, taking a nap in the sun or reading a book instead of forcing myself to make that phone call on my "to do" list. After letting it go, nine out of ten times the call will be unnecessary or when I do make the call it works in my favor. Synchronicities are all about flow, if something isn't flowing your wasting your precious time. Doing something different will usually reopen blocked energy and the synchronicities will start to flow again. If I don't get Angel parking in town (which I normally do) I know my timing is off. I will relax while driving around the block, enjoying the scenery looking for what *they* may want me to see. Nine times out of ten, I will come across something I have been looking for and get it at a bargain price, if not for free!

A woman who had trouble seeing these synchronicities came to me for a health-related issue, and her reading indicated that she needed to do something artistic to clear up blocked energy in her throat chakra. She happened to be very talented at painting, but had given it up. I intuitively felt that she must return to her passion. Furthermore, she also wanted to tackle a lower chakra goal: finding a way to make some extra money while staying at home. She put her chakra prescription off until one day her daughter had missed the bus. Frustrated, she hopped in the car to drive her daughter to school. In the course of doing so, she just happened to run into not one but three women that told her about a craft fair during the holiday season where she could exhibit her art. When she called me, she said she finally understood the whole synchronicity phenomenon. Maybe her daughter was "supposed" to miss the bus, so that the universe could encourage her to follow through with her prescription. What you need might be staring you in the face, if you would only pay attention to the quirky way the unseen world works.

Synchronicities alone will not ensure your success. Intentions can only come to fruition if we are willing to do the required homework and want to move forward. When a door opens, you have to have the courage to walk through it. Doing so only makes the synchronicities come more often and puts us back into the flow of life. Frustration is a sure sign of a blocked chakra system. Years ago, before I clearly understood the phenomenon of synchronicities, I laid out my intentions to manifest money for a new carpet in my home. The carpet I had was so old, it kept tearing apart and I would have to sew it back together, over and over again. One day after tripping over the carpet for the third time, frustrated and angry, I ripped the carpet up to expose a beautiful hardwood floor underneath. If I would have been paying more attention to the force and flow of life at that time I could have saved myself a lot of frustration and a whole lot of thread! Little did I know that the carpet was supposed to rip so that I could see what lay underneath. Also, the synchronicity would have been wasted unless I motivated myself to finish the job by disposing of the old carpet. *They* truly want to help you, so send out your intentions for positive change in your life... and when the synchronicities start to occur, break out of your comfort zone, trust the universe, and have fun manifesting your heart's true desires.

If one wants to grow spiritually, there is always homework to be done following a reading. I had one reading with a man who had stones only in his first and sixth chakra. He either lived in his head, reliving the past and worrying about the future, or was so tight with his money that people would call him a miser. You could say he was a real "stick in the mud" focusing primarily on material things and money. I prescribed spontaneously driving a different way home from work and taking a trip with his family, reopening his second chakra. He never took that trip and he still drives the same way home everyday from a job he hates. He goes home sits in the same chair, watching the same television show as he did last week, complains about the same things he did last year and wonders why his life never changes.

Einstein said, "Insanity is doing the same thing over and over again and expecting different results." I have prescribed letter-writing, belly dancing, buying flowers for yourself, riding a bike and going for a walk with your dog… some very simple prescriptions. Unfortunately, many find these little spiritual "pills" are too difficult to swallow. My grandmother use to say, "God helps those who help themselves." I say, "Spontaneity is the seed of synchronicity." It is very important to want change and to do the work needed to manifest the things you want into the physical world. Crystal Readings can identify areas of your life that may need some loving attention, but it is up to you to take the first step. Just do it and watch the synchronicities begin to effortlessly flow into your life.

"There is no future. There is only now. You can have all the hope in the future you want, but if you do not act now, nothing will come of it."-Rabbi Rami Shapiro

Dream Interpretation

More information simply makes a reading deeper and more meaningful. So far, I've discussed astrology, numerology, intuition, synchronicities, colors, and their relationship to the chakras. Now, let's talk about dreams, and what they can tell you about your participants. I believe that to dream is to live a second life, a life without physical form where we explore the ethereal realm using our highest chakras. We leave our bodies every night, returning in the morning to the physical world to be born again. We wake up and say, "it was only a dream", but the dream is real. It only seems as if it were an illusion because the ethereal realm is so intangible. If you have ever had a nightmare, and we all have, didn't the emotions feel just as genuine as they do in your *real* life? Listen to what your dreams are telling you, at least as much as you do to your waking experiences. You will then be enrolled as a fulltime student in the class of life. After all, "life is but a dream."

I encourage asking your participants about recurring and recent dreams, especially if you see a lot of stones in the higher chakras (6th and 7th). Dreams are a way for the mind to process excess energy. I call it "data dumping" from the past, all that stuff we witnessed but really didn't want to see in childhood or even as an adult. When we mindlessly allow ourselves to take in unhealthy information such as the evening news or violent movies, our energy is affected whether we are aware of it or not. Nightmares are a way for us to energetically "de-bug" our minds involuntarily. We can help this process along voluntarily by writing them down, discussing them, and finally interpreting their hidden meanings. I had a reading with a woman who chose three cracked purple stones and was afraid to fall asleep in fear of having the same recurring nightmare. She described the dreams to me, and her fear of experiencing them again and again. At that time in her life, she was in a safe place and had time to work through her past via these dreams. I told her that the more she allowed herself to experience and discuss them, the more she would get these frightening visions out of her head. Eventually, this would also clear up her sixth chakra. I believe that dreams are often messages, and a dream not interpreted is like a letter unread. What are "they" trying to tell you? If you are not already well trained in dream interpretation, there are many wonderful books available on the subject; I suggest you invest in one.

When I see too many sixth chakras stones I ask them about their dreams. If I see no stones, I know this person needs to dream, and when I see tainted stones I ask about nightmares. One good example of too many sixth chakra stones is a reading I had with a woman who said she dreamt that she went back to school and no one recognized her. Nobody new who she was and that frustrated her while she was dreaming. She had three stones in her 6th chakra, no power stones (3rd chakra) and had a nervous twitch in her left eye (mind/body), telling me that there was something she needed to see related to a woman. The reading revealed that she had spent her whole life living for her parents, her husband, and finally her children. Her kids were entering school and she was stressed, with no explanation. I asked her if she thought she knew who she truly was inside. She assured me she did! One hour later, at the conclusion of the reading, she stood up and said, "You know, I just need to find out who I really am". Her prescription was to spend time alone meditating on what she wanted for herself and to read lots of empowering books. She did just that, and it changed her life.

"To accomplish great things, we must dream as well as act."-Anatole France

Making "Dreams" Come True

When it comes to getting what you desire, intentions are everything. Everything we physically produce in this world starts in our heads as a thought. You can call it hope, a dream or a prayer. These are just examples of communicating with the intangible world by making your desires known. It's like knocking on the door of the unseen universe and then waiting for it to open. The Angels, your guides, the universe or God, whatever you choose to call them/it, are waiting to assist you.

Years ago I sent my intentions (7th crown chakra) out into the universe about a specific place I wanted to work. One night, I had a dream with Yoko Ono, very pregnant, and ready to give birth. In the other room, lay John Lennon at his funeral. The dream told me that something was going to begin, or be born, while something else would end, or pass away.

At that time in my life, I had a dream of working at this beautiful and exclusive health club in my neighborhood, but I lacked the self- esteem to approach anyone at the club about a job. I was afraid (fight or flight 1st chakra), but my guides said to me "just do it." When I heard the whisper and remembered my dream, (intuition 6th chakra), I suddenly felt a strong commitment to be true to myself (self love 4th chakra). I went in (3rd power chakra), asked for a job (5th throat chakra), and was hired that day. Trusting in the universe was definitely part of the equation for getting what I desired, but what actually landed me the job was my passion for dancing, exercise, and teaching. My heart-felt intentions were to do what I loved for a living.

The same day I had the courage to walk in, everyone else had gotten fired! I worked there for years and I loved it! I called it my *dream* job. If I still had power issues or deserving issues, I may not have listened to the dream or to my inner voice and could have missed out on the perfect situation! I asked through prayer involving the crown chakra, and then the sixth chakra kicked in with my dream and my intuitive voice, moving me to ask with the fifth chakra for the job. Deserving the new job was made possible by the self-love in my fourth chakra. My power and courage arose from my third. Trusting myself to follow through and not chicken out is the second chakra. Ultimately showing up physically to do the job, was using my root chakra.

Constructive thoughts help us get what we truly want in a tangible form. Ask and you shall receive! If all chakras are flowing, I will think deserving thoughts and then I can find the strength to walk through doors when the universe holds them open for me.

> "Living twice at once you learn
> You are safe frrom pain in the dream domain
> A soul set free to fly
> A round trip journey in your head
> Master of illusion, can you realize
> Your dreams alive, you can be the guide."
> -Chris Degarmo, of Queensryche
> *Silent Lucidity*

Ending the Reading

When the reading is almost finished, I put both the crystals and my cards away, and ask them if they have any questions or comments. They will write their chakra prescriptions down (usually three) and end the reading with the drawing of an Angel card (the "fortune cookie" cards described previously). These cards work like magic. I have done readings for people who think that I have somehow "rigged" this deck. I once had a reading with a woman whose crystals revealed that she needed to nurture and develop compassion for herself. As she picked her Angel card, another slid out from the deck. I said she needed to read both of them. One card was entitled *compassion* and the other *nurture*. It all seems a little spooky, but after all these years, I now expect things like this! That is when the universe steps in and helps you help others. The woman who had been mourning her friend and needed to grieve, chose a card that read *hello from heaven* not once, but twice in consecutive readings! The card reads "Your loved ones in Heaven are doing fine. Let go of worries, and feel their loving blessings." (Doreen Virtue)

The last step of a reading is to give them a keepsake, which will remind them of their experience and the work they will continue. I ask them to pick a crystal to take with them (with their eyes closed). Most of my clients will choose a crystal related to one of the chakras that we have discussed, representing an issue that needs work or healing. And yes, I feel that this is another example of the that unseen energy which makes all of the "pieces" fit together and make sense – a power that sleeps within us all.

"Where the spirit does not work with the hand, there is no art." - Leonardo Davinci

Prescriptions for the Chakras

At the end of each reading, I come up with what I call a "chakra prescription." We discuss the chakra that needs the most help, and find something simple to jumpstart that energy center. If you feel that you suffer from such chakra deficiencies, I guarantee that if you do at least one thing different, the direction of your life will change.

Different activities will stimulate different Chakras. For example, if I want to open my heart chakra, I could write a love letter to the person of my dreams, even if I haven't met them yet. If I felt my throat chakra was suffering from a blockage, then taking an art or singing class could be the perfect prescription. When chakras are too open, balance is the remedy. If you have an excessive power chakra let someone else drive. If you are around people all the time (sacral chakra), spend time alone. When a chakra is too open, the prescription is do the opposite of what you would normally do... Here are a few examples of chakra **opening** prescriptions that I have used in my readings. One a day could keep the doctor away!

Chakra	Prescription
First *Chakra* Survival	Walk in nature, eat meat, plant a garden, sleep in, sit still, pay your monthly bills early. Slow down! Hike up a mountain. Hug a tree. Feel your roots. Clean your house, eat healthy foods, and walk outside with bare feet. Do nothing. Plant a tree. Take a vacation in nature. Go bird watching and admire the animals in nature. Play the drums, do yoga. Wear red. Eat red foods and protein.
Second *Chakra* Relationships	Take a bath, sit by water, stretch, swim, move your hips, dance, feel what others feel, drink liquids. Be sexual. Do something spontaneous. Go to the ocean. Join a group that you have an interest in, take a class for fun. Adopt a pet. Volunteer with children or the elderly. Make a new friend. Drive somewhere you have never been. Start a group. Go on a retreat with people you don't know. Listen to Latin music and salsa dance. Wear orange. Eat orange foods and drink liquids.
Third *Chakra* Empowerment	Laugh, skip, swing, cry, run, breathe, move your body forward, watch a fire and burn stuff. Take up the martial arts, Tai Chi or boxing. Take an aerobic class, lift weights. Ride a bike like a child again. Hit balls at the batting cage or golf range and think of issues that anger you and let them go with each hit. Play a competitive sport. March in a parade. Wear Yellow. Eat yellow food and starches.
Fourth *Chakra* Connection	Hold hands, talk about how you feel. Buy flowers and date yourself. Talk or smile at a stranger. Tell someone you love them. Play a game with your family. Volunteer in your community. Love someone for no reason at all! Get a massage. Look in the mirror and say you love yourself just the way you are. Send yourself a valentine. Learn Reiki (healing touch) listen to Gregorian chants. Wear pink or green. Eat green food and vegetables.

Fifth *Chakra* *Expression*	Sing, write, draw, play an instrument, paint, work with clay or wood. Talk to someone you trust. Go to a festival with music and art. Start a band. Karaoke. Journal, chant or do a mantra. Read poetry, write a song, visit the museum. Support the arts in your community. Be in a play. Teach something you love to do to someone you care about. Verbally pass down a family tradition. Write a letter, or attend an Opera. Wear blue. Eat blue foods and fruit.
Sixth *Chakra* *Intuition*	Guess someone's sign, listen to your intuition, write down your dreams, imagine, daydream and fantasize. Read positive books, watch uplifting movies. Believe in something you can't see. Guess who it is when the phone rings. See yourself in a brighter future. Brainstorm about yourself and your desires, if you had all the time, money and freedom what would you do? Listen to classical music like Mozart. Wear purple. Eat purple foods and breathe.
Seventh *Chakra* *Knowing*	Connect with a higher power, talk to an Angel, meditate, be still, listen, trust your inner knowing, belong and connect with others. Think lofty thoughts. Prophesize about the future! Ask questions and ponder. Look at the stars. Pray for yourself and others. Write down your goals and ask your higher self to help you achieve them. Think positive affirmations. Listen to music from India. Wear violet or white. Eat white foods or fast.

Trinity: "No one has ever done anything like this."
Neo: "That's why its going to work."
-The Warshowski Brothers, *The Matrix*

Example Crystal Reading

The participant is a Gemini (cardinal and masculine), an air sign representing freedom and communication. Her life number is an eight, suggesting that this life is about learning to use the lower chakras: power and abundance (3rd and 1st chakra, respectively). Surprisingly, when I look at the chosen stones, I see that she is missing the lower three chakras. There are two expression stones (5th chakra) one is a nice clear blue and the other is cracked. She is intuitive (6th chakra, an amethyst) but not following her intuition (the second is shattered) and she has a great connection to the universe (7th chakra, moonstone). Her heart chakra stones are pink: one is healthy, representing self-love, but the other is stained and cracked (4th chakra). The broken pink stone says that her loss of connection could be associated with a woman. She needs to have free-flowing communication with this person, and she knows this, but unconsciously stops thinking about it when the idea surfaces because she lacks the courage to speak to her. When asked, she says she often has a sore throat and headaches (5th and 6th chakra). Interestingly, she admits to being afraid to speak up to her mother about something that has been weighing on her mind for a long time.

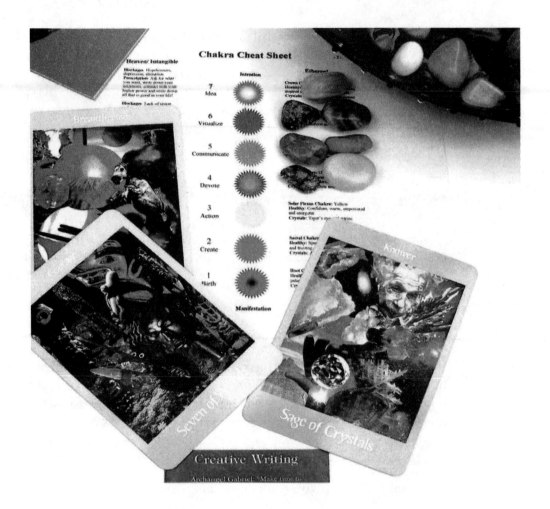

Her first card chosen was *knower*, second *courage* and the third card was *breakthrough*. The cards usually tell a story and go with what we discuss during the reading. She **knows** that she would like to get the issue off of her mind, and she is also aware that she is afraid, and needs some **courage** to do so. We discussed her writing it down and getting it out of her head. She then picked the *breakthrough* card. When the reading was ending she drew the Angel card, *creative writing*. It confirmed that writing down her feelings associated with her mother, and getting the issue off of her mind and chest may be the **breakthrough** she so desperately needed to get past her heart chakra, accessing her lower power chakra.

Her year number is 22/4, and this is the most powerful year number. It is now or never! A *four* year…the more you give the more you get! She has to assert herself and muster up the courage to express her feelings honestly and freely with her mother. Communication is so important to a Gemini, and her prescription would be to write down everything that she would like to say to her mother to jump-start her throat chakra (I wouldn't advise giving it to her mother just yet, future readings would determine that). I also would recommend something physical. For example, a kickboxing class or running may help her get out of her head and back into the lower chakras. Speaking her mind and expressing herself freely with the people around her will make this 22/4 year very powerful and abundant.

ourage is not the absence of fear, but the ability to walk through it."-Unknown

Readings with Multiple People: Relationship Readings

Learning about the people you love can positively enhance your relationships, and it can actually be a lot of fun. Relationship Readings help open lines of communication that may get severed the longer you live with someone, especially if there is a lack of understanding between the two of you. When we are seeking out the missing parts of ourselves, we attract certain people into our relationships: friends, lovers, and coworkers. They all mirror back to us the very thing we are searching for. Most couples exhibit directly opposite characteristics, as if both people fit together like a jigsaw puzzle. However, this complimentary nature of relationships is not always beneficial. I know a couple that are fire and water and it just never seems to work. They may be better off as friends! A happy couple can become burned out when someone in the relationship is always grounded and the other is "in the clouds." Meeting somewhere in the middle will always benefit both individuals, whether it is your spouse, child, coworker or a family member. Understanding your differences is the key to reaching this middle ground. When we enter into relationships as whole and healthy individuals, it is a recipe for a lifetime of success.

I developed my Relationship Readings practicing on a new love I met five years ago. I could see right away that we were drawn together to learn about our complimentary strengths and weaknesses. He was very intellectual, liked to make money and was very responsible. I, on the other hand, was spontaneous, social and carefree. He was a full blown "head first" Aries and I was the quintessential freedom-loving Gemini, I loved his heat and he loved my oxygen. You can imagine what kind of combustion we could have if you brought our two elements together without some type of control.

We knew from the readings that I felt too much and he was too logical. When arguing, I would overcompensate for his blocked heart with my empathetic 2nd chakra. He would shut down his feelings, igniting my orange chakra with tears and his power chakra with anger. When we were good we were great, and when we went untamed we were awful… like a fire out of control. We learned to communicate (5th chakra), which is so important for a Gemini. He learned to open his heart and feel, instead of over-intellectualizing like an Aries. The readings taught us about our differences, helping us to understand one another on so many different levels, and allowed us to grow together.

Seeing relationships as learning experiences is so empowering. That is one of the reasons we are here, to develop and evolve… through our relationships. Over time, I have come to work a little harder, use my logic instead of emotions and not to take things so personally. He has opened his heart, gotten in touch with his anger and learned to dance spontaneously without me asking. We have both learned the importance of the power chakra by helping each other release some of our childhood issues. We did most of this together through some awesome 5th chakra communication, which is the only chakra we had working for us in the beginning. If we had not been aware of our energy exchange and continued along that path, I would have become the submissive female and he would have maintained his domineering male role. We would have been so out of balance that I could have literally called my "other half." When we would get together for a "session" with my crystals, it not only benef energetically, it helped me use all of my chakras to manifest one of my "ah ha!" moments… crea developing Relationship Readings. This is what our chakras looked like when we started journey together:

Our Relationship Reading

		HERS	HIS

7th   *Logic*

6th   *Intuition*

5th   *Communication*

4th   *Self-Love*

3rd   *Power and Control*

2nd   *Relationships*

1st   *Stability*

56

You can see that our chakras fit like puzzle pieces; our stones in an individual reading would look much different. Our only connection was at our throat chakras. Over time, we had many Crystal Readings. He is still working on maintaining an open heart and my homework is to keep my feet on the ground. We are balanced now and experience more harmony together. Our energy really does matter! I call it "Coupling Therapy," bringing two energies together for optimal flow! Being on the same page as a couple, and working toward a common vision, allows us to easily manifest our dreams together.

Getting Started

Relationship Readings are done with the couple sitting side-by-side, across from me. I ask each person to write down their name and birthday (that helps when you are doing many readings in a day and have trouble remembering all the names). I tell them their signs and explain the astrological similarities and differences. Our differences make us who we are and I feel we choose everything about our lives to learn certain lessons.

As each person chooses their stones, I look for quirks in their behavior. I watch and see if they fight over a crystal or if they put one back. I lay their stones out next to each other starting with the first chakra and moving up to the seventh, and like the one-on-one readings, I examine the stones they have chosen. I take note of what chakras look healthy between the two and discuss them. Then I explain the blocks they may have together. Giving them positive feedback is the most important thing you can do. You always have to be encouraging and see the glass full! If all the crystals were opposite I would never say, "What are you two doing together?" Instead, I would ask, "what do you have to offer each other?" I feel that **fortune** telling should be about telling people how **fortunate** they are.

As with individual readings, you can draw information from many different sources. For instance, a couple's year cycles are very important. If one is in a "1" cycle and the other in a "6" cycle, they may be in conflict over various life decisions (moving, changing jobs, and having children). Also, look deeper into the characteristics of the astrological signs. Cardinal signs like to lead while other signs need to be led. "Organizers" can irritate some signs and be respected by others. For instance, a Sagittarius is a mutable fire sign and is masculine, not very predictable. A Taurus is a fixed earth sign and is feminine, very predictable. These signs would become very aggravated with one another if they had to work side by side on a project. If these signs were married, I would go into detail about their differences and probably advise them to go see a mediator so they could find constructive ways to work together. These two signs may be seeking in each other what on an individual level they are missing in themselves. You have to be a detective and put all the pieces together. This helps answer the questions "why have we been attracted to each other?" "What is our lesson?" and "How do we build upon what we already have?"

If I do a reading with a couple and find that they are not satisfied with each other, I have them write down what they expect from their mate. They will make a lengthy list, and when asked if they see all of those qualities in themselves, they will most likely answer, "no." How can you expect certain virtues from someone else when you've never had them within yourself? Since Rome was not built in a day, we go back to the crystals and pick a single chakra to work on. It could be more heart-felt communication with their partner, or even more laughter. The prescription for that reading could be a night out at a quiet restaurant where they each read a poem expressing how they feel, ending the evening with a comedy show. It is that simple!

My favorite readings are with couples whose progress you can follow over time. Watching people grow is so inspiring! Even the most perfect relationships are built on both work and play, striking a balance between the two. Changing and evolving as a team is a natural progression. I did a particularly satisfying Valentine's Day reading for one of my favorite couples. They are truly soul mates, a fact that was obvious to me the moment I met them. Yet, like any couple, each had issues that needed proper attention. They both had issues to work on relating to their childhood conditioning. He was too responsible and she too needy. She loved to talk and express herself while he would hold his words inside to spare her feelings. The reading pointed to some problems in the relationship, such as working opposite shifts. They were growing apart due to the lack of quality time spent together. The stones and cards revealed that it would benefit their relationship tremendously if they could be together during the day even if it was a planned *date*. After sharing their strengths and weaknesses in the reading, they reached a new level of understanding, becoming much closer. Two weeks later, I heard through the grapevine that he had quit his job and found something totally new so they could spend more time together. He trusted the universe and took a chance, re-opening his second chakra. I call that *free falling*.

You'll find that people will be drawn to the same stones over and over again, even if they are sticking to their prescriptions, because positive change takes time. However, they may seem to change overnight if something dramatic has happened to them recently. For example, a fight with a spouse or loved one, marriage, or loss of one's job can change the stones of someone with previously consistent readings. A year after their first reading, the same couple I mentioned earlier came to me because their lives were about to change on many levels. They were getting married, wanting to have a child and moving to Australia. Normally, this is more stress than most relationships can take at once. They both had quit their jobs for the move and were having major financial problems. She was a fire sign, with enough passion to ignite an icicle. He was a thoughtful and responsible water sign, having an "all or nothing" attitude. As a result of all this stress and confusion, they had pulled away from one another and were losing their greatest asset: their communication with one another. I had them write down what they most loved about each other when they first met. They read their descriptions out loud and you could see love rekindled in their eyes! She remembered that she was drawn to him because of his dependability and warm heart. He, on the other hand, was drawn to her for her spontaneous, playful, and talkative nature.

Their stones agreed with their personalities, but further revealed troubles they were facing. Both were in a "defensive" stance, reacting to their situation. His stones revealed his stress and closed heart. Her stones showed she had lost her ability to communicate, and felt some heartbreaking issues surfacing from her past. Both were playing out childhood dramas on one another. He wanted to handle the money, throwing water on her newly lit fire. However, she had lived without financial security her whole life and in discovering she finally could make her own way, wasn't about to relinquish that independence. He was saying: "my way, or no way," and the two were involved in a tug of war.

During the reading, she drew the *passion* and the *sun* card, while he drew the *achiever* and the *emperor* card. He wanted to be the father and she wanted to be the spontaneous child. To make their relationship last, they would have to work together. They agreed that he would have to learn to play and she would have to get down to business. Then, she pulled the *reflection* card and I felt it was related to the new baby they were trying to conceive. She agreed to wait a month after they were married before adding more to their plate.

He drew the *compassion* card, which said he needed to feel again, putting himself in her shoes. He agreed, seeing that he needed to relax and worry less about everything and share the responsibility as a couple. He had stopped the flow to his heart and that was shutting down their heartfelt communication that she thrived on, a kind of unconscious punishment from him. His reading revealed some pain from his childhood caused by his father, and it was causing him grief at this time in his life because he felt the need to step into his father's shoes. It was time to live his life with his fiancé and let go of parenting the people around him. When discussing his childhood, he made a comment on how his mother needed to learn to relax and quit taking care of others. I had him stand in front of the mirror, look himself in the eye and make the same statement, saying his name instead of his mother's. He had to tell himself to relax and quit taking care of others. Again, we choose the people in our lives, teaching us various lessons, so that we may ultimately choose ourselves. That reading helped them both individually, and as a couple. They chose each other to learn valuable lessons and they are growing together. While writing this book, I received an email about their Australian fairy tale wedding, two new life-affirming occupations and the announcement of a new baby.

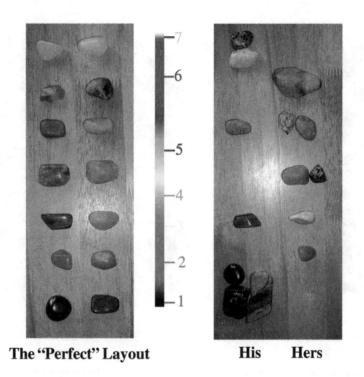

The "Perfect" Layout   **His   Hers**

Laid side by side, the stones usually look like a like a jigsaw puzzle. The participants are drawn together to help balance what each is missing in their chakra system. In a healthy relationship, we learn about those missing traits from the other person and change accordingly to grow both individually and together. In this reading, the man is carrying the financial burden. He worries too much and his heart is closed. She is very imaginative and talkative. Her heart is open, but reveals pain with a man (green stone with black specks); she feels powerless (tainted yellow stone) and needs nurturing. He is drawn to her Sagittarius warmth, compassion and spontaneity and she is drawn to his stable father-like dependability. He could learn to be more flexible and carefree (second chakra), and she could take more responsibility (first chakra) and learn to listen more attentively to what he has to say with out taking it personally.

I do Relationship Readings not only for couples, but also to help family members learn more about each other on an energetic level. I had an interesting reading with a mother and her daughter. The mother was concerned with the daughter's schoolwork and wanted some insight on how she might motivate her daughter to focus on her homework. However, it became clear in the reading that the mom needed to do some homework of her own. She had been living an "all work, no play" scenario for so long it was stressing her daughter out. Every night after work, the mom would arrive home, already stressed, and stand over her daughter and figuratively force her nose to the grindstone. The young girl was even enrolled in a very expensive school for additional instruction at night. It was clear to me that the mother needed to loosen her grip on her familiar authoritarian attitude, and try doing things a bit differently. The mom's "homework" was to daydream more, and to give her daughter some space to work alone in her room. After a couple of readings, the mother decided to spend some creative time by herself through taking a stain-glass window class. Changing her normal behavior allowed them both to grow in ways that improved their relationship. Can you guess whose crystals are whose? Clue: The mom is too grounded and the daughter lives in her head. Notice the mothers heart stones, can you tell from whom she may have picked up her "all work, no play" scenario?

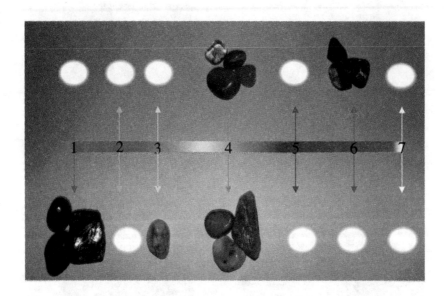

In this fast-paced and chaotic world, many of us have forgotten how to love both one another and ourselves. Many of us have forgotten how to treat our body with the respect that it so deserves. We have forgotten the balance between work and play, as well as how to be creative, passionate and loving. Remembering to take time to daydream, fantasize, or to sit silently while listening to the wind is so important to our inner health. It is equally beneficial to remember to stay grounded, focused and productive in the physical world, while remembering our connectedness to one another, reinforcing our love for humanity, and expressing our unique divine spirituality. Without these things in our lives, we become unbalanced and can inadvertently "bury" parts of ourselves that yearn to be free! The longer these parts stay buried, the greater the overload and potential for disease (see the following section). Bringing these parts to the surface is what Crystal Readings are all about. I am always surprised what issues come up and how they can affect our bodies. The more you know about yourself the more empowered you will be!

"Our thoughts and actions control our lives and can be altered to change our lives."
-James Redfield *The Celestine Prophecy*

The Mind/Body Connection

I find that Crystal Readings reopen the door to creative expression and self-love. I feel the most important way to nurture total health and wellbeing is through free-flowing self-expression. If we grew up repressing who we are to please others, and never change this behavior, we will pay for it in the end with our emotional health, eventually manifesting in our physical bodies. We are no longer held captive to our past; we learn from it and feel the power to be our true selves. We, as adults, can make appropriate changes to rectify this behavior and reclaim our future... We may have to break free of certain unhealthy habits, relationships or situations, and **only then** do we have the power to live the life we desire.

I use the "your life is a garden" metaphor within my readings. Would you consciously let a weed take over what you have planted? Would you plant seeds that say, "toxic" on the package? Focus on what you want and nurture those relationships, habits and situations that allow your garden to bloom. I have a *three strikes your out* rule. I give everyone I meet three chances to be in my garden. Most people I attract are energetically planted right away and come with a wheelbarrow full of synchronicities. Others come into my life to teach me something and mirror me so I can learn more about myself. They will uproot themselves once I have learned the lesson. My paradigm will shift a little and those people will usually weed themselves out of my life. Have you ever noticed the same type of person coming into your life over and over again? Are these people weeds in your garden? Look at what these people may be teaching you, and make the internal changes the universe is pushing for, and go back to planting roses!

"Positive growth requires effort and the will to change."-Unknown

Physical Clues

Present day health researchers would argue both for and against the fact that there exists a strong connection between the wellness of the mind and health of the body. When viewed from personal experiences, though, it comes as no surprise to many of us that accumulated negative emotions have caused physical discomfort, pain, and even disease. In fact, most of the readings that I do are about health-related issues. I use this mind-body connection, in a metaphoric sense, to help me figure out the types of negative emotions that my clients must resolve, based on the symptoms that arise in their bodies.

Looking at physical clues can give you a great deal of information. I have seen women with actual indents in their back and chest areas, indicating to me that they have been pulling their heart chakra in to protect themselves. Excess weight can serve as armor so watch where people tend to carry extra inches. That can be a chakra giveaway. Where are they losing hair? The top of the head could mean the crown chakra and the receding hairline could point to a blockage in the sixth chakra. Reading someone's body language can be an entire discipline in itself. Many books have been written on the subject, and would require more pages than I have space for to afford proper coverage in this book. However, I suggest paying close attention to obvious signs, such as when it seems that people "bear the weight of the world on their shoulders." Could it be that someone close to them is a "pain in the neck?" Look at the crystals and the condition of their body, then ask them what is going on with health-related issues and you may have your *three strikes your in* scenario.

When I see people cross their arms in front of their chest or stomach area I know that they may be protecting their heart or power chakras. People who look up a lot while talking have open third eyes. You can almost see them looking at their own movie in their mind's eye. Watch hand gestures: touching their heart, throat or head points to open chakras. Eye contact, posture and skin tone can also be indicators. I did a reading with a woman who looked pale and lifeless and gazed down at the ground a lot. When I looked at her crystals, she had all the lower surviving life stones and a couple heart stones that were dark and spotted. I knew life was bringing her down and she needed some energy pumped back into her heart. I asked what she loved to do as a child. She said "nothing," and I said, "how about as a teenager, anything you loved and no longer do?" She looked at me and said, "I use to dance". Her eyes brightened and her hair went back. She actually put color back in her face by thinking of dancing. Her prescription was easy to see.

I believe all disease starts in the unseen world first. I feel that poor health is connected to our internal thoughts and fears, and the physical world reflects how we think. My most enlightening reading was with a woman suffering from a brain disorder. Her crystals drew attention to her heart area, her power chakra and to her third eye. Her chest was sunken and her forehead cringed when she spoke of her mother. Intuitively, it seemed as though she had an issue with her mother from her past. I asked if she needed to get something off her chest, possibly related to her mother, maybe an issue that had been "weighing" on her mind. The answer was profound: a secret about her childhood she had never told anyone. I helped her reopen her power, heart and third eye chakras by allowing her to see in her mind's eye that she could assert herself with her mother. I call it a "do over," empowering her to change the outcome of a painful incident and enabling her to let go of her heartbreaking past. She was tested that same month when she called the clinic to get the results of her brain scan. They told her that she would have to wait a month for her appointment to get the results. Remembering that her prescription was to assert herself, she told the woman at the clinic she wouldn't wait and that she wanted the test results now! The woman gave her the good news on the phone that same day. Asserting yourself takes practice and the lessons we must learn usually come in threes. I am sure she will have to be assertive with a woman two more times before she really passes this test with flying colors!

Embracing self-love by asserting yourself is one of the most powerful lessons we can learn. I had given many readings to a man who had his throat chakra closed. He played the guitar, sang and wrote his own songs. Clearly he was using his self-expression, opening his throat chakra through his music. However, it is one thing to express your mind, it is another thing entirely to express your heart. We talked about his childhood, delving into his feelings while he was growing up. He had experienced tremendous sadness, strife, and struggle as a youth, with no way of emoting to someone close by. He was an only child and never really developed enough of a connection with anyone to share his own feelings verbally. In his first reading, he revealed to me that he thought constantly that he wanted to kill himself. His prescription was to write a song about his children and to us the mantra "I choose life!" The irony of these sessions is that he too, was diagnosed with a brain tumor about sixth months after our first reading. The tumor was located at the base of his brain, directly behind his fifth chakra, where I saw such a powerful blockage months before.

In previous readings, I could see a past life that was affecting him still today, a life where he was paralyzed from the neck down. He was helpless, yet revered by many. I saw that these people who cared for him carried him around on a platform on their shoulders, so that he could spread wisdom to his people. He must have been a very wise and knowledgeable man. I asked him what he did for a living now, and he said he had started a business called Steps Inc., a service that helps disabled individuals get out of their homes to do errands. All of his readings revealed that his higher chakras were overactive. Yet, one of his readings revealed that all of his chakras were represented and healthy. I asked what he had been doing prior to our reading. He said he had been taking a walk in the woods. It was clear to me that he was an Aries who needed to get back into his body. His head was even measured to be a size bigger than his torso would lead you to believe. He told me that, in the reserves, they had to get him a special helmet for his large head. I believed that to be a carry over from his past life.

By connecting his present life with his past life, I had a new insight into his current condition. I found it meaningful that he may have felt indebted to those people in his past life who carried him for so many years. Now, he felt he was paying the world back through his business. Subsequent sessions centered on him asserting himself with others, or "putting his foot down," using his fifth chakra to say "No!" The most important lesson he learned was, like the woman who asked for her test results, being more assertive and speaking up for himself. He was supposed to go into surgery to have his tumor removed, but thought "I could take a walk in the woods or get my head cut open"… reluctantly, he chose to have surgery. His first physician discussed making an incision at the top of his head and splitting his brain in half to get to the tumor, carrying the possible side effect of developing symptoms associated with Parkinson's disease: shaking and trembling. To this procedure, he said "No!" A second physician discussed another type of surgery, which involved taking a much different path through the brain. Unfortunately, one of the many side effects of this procedure could be paralysis, a definite connection to his past life! Again, he said "NO!" Finally, a third surgeon suggested a far less invasive procedure with less chance of side effects, to which he said, "OK." He is now free of the brain tumor and is taking the needed "steps" to give to himself as much as he has given to others.

If we hold onto painful experiences from our past they can literally "eat us up" inside if we don't let them go. If you stumble upon something big when giving a reading, let your client talk it out and always have tissues close by. Tears are a great way to emote and when you are done with the reading you could suggest counseling, or a support group affiliated with their issue. Helping people uncover core issues is a process that isn't affected by time, and is often completely guided by intuition. I have given readings that have lasted up to three hours. I have thought about using a timer, but intuitively, I can't do it. The universe doesn't recognize our time or limitations. On the spiritual side, everything is perfect. What if I had stopped five minutes short of helping a client uncover their core issue? I have run into people, after a year, who tell me how touched they were with only one reading and how it changed their life. You cannot put a price on compassion! I do have to be honest and say that occasionally during a reading my ego will cloud my vision and say, "you should charge extra for this reading," and *they* will say, "relax and let us drive!" I am always amazed in the end.

"As the mind clears, the eyes see more." -Unknown

Everyone has something they would like to get off their chest. Each one of us has something trapped inside, and we often wish for someone to draw it out of us. Think of it as "spiritual surgery." Everyone for whom I have done readings has always felt relieved after sharing something previously locked inside. The mind has the ability to help the body heal through positive emotions. Yet, negative emotions can be detrimental to our health. Anger, guilt, sadness, or whatever the emotion; the crystals will verify which chakra is involved.

Shame can be held in the third chakra, grief in the fourth, and guilt in the second. Storing negative energies in these chakras will throw the body out of balance. By letting go of the past, we can easily move toward the future. However, if we wallow in the injustices done to us, we will pay the price for it in the long run. Letting go or holding on to negative emotions is a conscious choice. If we take the time to get to know what is holding us back and throwing us off balance, we can release it and have a healthy and happy life.

We get headaches because we train ourselves to forget. When suppressed thoughts arise, we push them back down. Eventually we close our heart, are unable to feel, and get heart-related issues like high blood pressure and heart disease. If we hold emotions in, we may have bowel problems that could lead to cancer, especially if carcinogens are allowed to sit and fester in your body. If we have been holding words back in fear of the people around us, then we may have thyroid problems or sore throats. Our bodies are perfect and will also behave accordingly to our thoughts about them. If we say, "my stomach is killing me," you are probably right! If you say, "I am sick and tired of my ex-wife" you are more than likely having a psychic moment.

When reading the crystals, it is important to ask the right questions. If I see too many stones in the third chakra, I will ask if they have stomach issues. If there is an imbalance in the sacral chakra, it could be female disorders, while the heart area could point to blood pressure problems, and the head could suggest migraines. Whatever the stones show, I ask questions and open up conversation so they can talk about their health. What can they do to help their situation? Why have they been holding back? Who are they allowing to stop them from living their life the way they want? Readings can open up their minds to changing their lifestyles and treating themselves with respect. In the end, it is all about self-love and what we can do to show ourselves how magnificent we truly are!

An example of a reading that has a bearing on health issues might go as follows: A man has two tainted black stones (1st chakra), three power stones (3rd chakra) one being a mustarded color, one broken throat (5th chakra) and a cracked dyed third eye stone (6th chakra). He is missing his connection to the universe (7th chakra), heart (4th chakra) and family nurturing stones (2nd chakra). I would first ask about ulcers and heart problems. He has too much energy stored below the heart. I would also look at his hair to see if he is balding, and if so, where? Balding at the crown of the head indicates a loss of a spiritual connection and a receding hairline, analyzing or over intellectualizing. The 1st and 3rd chakras have five stones represented, this may indicate that money and power may be too important to this individual and it may be killing his relationships. The heart chakra is the most important of the chakra system, and these stones are missing. This person needs spiritual CPR! With no heart stones, I know they have no feelings for others due to past trauma. This could be a person raised with violence in the home and absolutely no heart-felt expression in his life. This person has protected his heart in the past but needs to feel again.

I would have them write down five major incidences in their life, and I would then ask them their feelings that went with the experiences. Many times they will say, "I think," and never, without coaxing, say the words "I feel!" This reading says that this person could take over another country and still sleep at night, eventually dying of a heart attack in the middle of his so called restful sleep. I would recommend one-on-one counseling to open up communication and a team sport like hockey or football that would release the anger built up from his past. Recently I have seen wartime veterans with this exact layout. They went away to do their jobs as soldiers, and in the process, were forced to close down their third eye, their hearts, and their connection with others (feminine chakras). Survival (1st) and power (3rd), both masculine chakras, had to overcompensate for these blockages. The cards in his reading were *Negativity, Change* and *Passion.* Can you see what *They* were trying to tell him? Reconnecting with others (2nd chakra individual counseling and a team sport), thus finding balance within his feminine/masculine chakras, is his new mission.

Masculine and Feminine

The sides of the body have masculine and feminine qualities. Left is feminine and right is masculine. These are powerful clues to guide you to what your participants are feeling. For instance, if I see a man with deafness in his left ear I will ask how communication is going with his wife. If a woman comes to me and has issues with her right ovary I would ask if she has some great idea that her husband doesn't support. I know a man who had his left pinky in a cast, I asked him if he was carrying a burden with his family associated with a woman and he said his wife was in school and she was almost finished. He would be relieved soon of the financial burden. I also had a reading with a woman who had a cast on the very same pinkie finger. She was running a family business where everyone around her depended on her for their livelihoods.

The masculine and feminine qualities of the right and left sides don't always point to the person causing the issue. It can also suggest the nature of the problem. For instance, shouldering a burden can be a very masculine-oriented issue. Left can represent the *yin* or feminine receptive qualities, and right *yang* represents outgoing projecting qualities. I can guarantee that my right shoulder will act up when I start shouldering other people's problems. My right shoulder is my barometer to stop and take some time for myself and allow others to carry their own weight. Another sign for me is my self expression, have you ever noticed how many people have sore throats after the Holidays?

I did a reading with a young boy at the age of 12. His main concern was that he was short. I had no idea where this reading would take us, but we moved forward with the choosing of the crystals. He had all of his stones below his heart and had one of my worry stones in his 1st chakra. I asked him if he worried a lot, his reply was "yes" I asked him to write some of them down. One of his major concerns was with death and that his mother would die. He thought about it constantly. I took the time to talk about death with him and afterwards, he felt like a weight had lifted off his mind. The reading was a success. Who would have thought he was spending so much time in his mind on the subject of death? It only got better when a month later he started to grow, first his shoe size and then in height, he even slimmed down and became more active. The next year you wouldn't have known him as the same boy, he was looking more like a young man. The pituitary gland is located in the 6th chakra and these stones were missing. His worrying could have been cutting off important growth hormones he needed in puberty.

Glands, and the chakras associated with them, are another way to view energy. The throat chakra and the thyroid are connected. I have had many women in readings that showed no throat stones and have had their thyroids removed. The adrenal gland is another one that is taxed when we are always afraid and living only in the fight or flight 1st chakra. I had a woman in her 70s tell me that she always thought when she retired at 65 her life would be over. She had diabetes, and I asked her when she contracted it, to which she told me "sixty-five." Her pancreas had been listening, and at 65, all the joy had been squeezed out of her life. I asked her what she enjoyed to do before she retired? She said she used to love to sing and dance, can you guess what her prescription might have been?

I knew a woman who had major dental work done, costing her too much for her to ever pay back. I asked her if she wanted to have a reading with me. She thought about it for a while, and eventually came in when she was ready. Her fifth chakra stones were tainted and she had lost her ability to dream or see the good in her life. Bruxism (teeth grinding or clenching while sleeping) was the cause of her dental problems, keeping her mouth shut and holding her tongue over many years. We discussed her childhood and wrote down five things she would like to have said to her parents. After the reading, she said she was going to open up conversation with her father about how she felt. She followed through with her chakra prescriptions and after doing so, received the money for the dental bills for her birthday from her parents. Birthdays are new beginnings, and since that reading, she has continued to express herself to the people around her.

"It is a wise mans part, rather to avoid sickness, than to wish for medicines."
-Thomas More, *Utopia*

The significance of right and left are the best clues to help understand heart-related issues. If I see the heart chakra with a tainted pink stone, and the participant's left shoulder is lower than their right, I know to ask about a woman in their life. If I see a right knee problem and a tainted green stone in the heart chakra, I will ask them about issues in changing direction with a man, pivoting back and forth without moving forward. You may have to take notes when you start out and look up the meaning later. The mind/body connection is metaphoric and only a small part of the reading, so only use it when it applies. Remember you are not a doctor, and never give medical advice. Educate them on their energetic bodies and on their chakra systems only.

Index of Mind/Body Metaphors and the Chakras
(Adapted in part from Louise Hay's *You Can Heal Your Life*)

Left Side of the body-receptivity, taking in, feminine energy, woman/mother/yin
Right side of the body- giving out, letting go, masculine energy, man/father/yang

The number in parentheses () signifies the associated chakra

Adrenal- doing too much, burned out, stressed, fight or flight (1)
Ankle- unable to change, flexibility in changing directions in life, indecision (1)
Anus- letting go of past hurts, holding on to negative emotions (1)
Arms- heart related, receptive to being loved, giving and receiving (4)
Arteries- life affirming, receiving love, joy, happiness, the ability to flow with life (4)
Back- lack of support, issues in the past, responsibility
      Low- money, financial worries, lack of support (2)
      Middle- lack of love for self, pain from the past, broken hearted (4)
      Upper- heavy burdens, weight of the world on your shoulders, too responsible (5)
Bladder- letting go of old emotions, releasing feelings (2)
Blood- life, giving, flowing, nourishment (4)
Bones- structure, balance, standing strongly for oneself, spineless (1)
Bowels- holding on to unresolved issues, releasing built up emotions over time (1)
Brain- the body's computer, who is in control? (7)
Breasts- mothering, nurturing, giving (4)
Buttocks- power, strength, girth, presence (1)
Ears- listening, understanding, hearing (6)
Elbow- ability to give and nurture self and others, flexibility in giving to oneself (4)
Eyes- windows of the soul, perception, awareness (6&7)
Face- what you show the world, identity, self esteem, your façade (5&6)
Feet- standing up for yourself, foundation, stepping forward (1)
Fingers- taking, giving, grasping
      Thumb- power and holding ability, strength (3)
      Index- blaming, not taking responsibility, pointing the finger (1)
      Middle- anger, sexuality (2)
      Ring- unions, the love or lack of (4)
      Pinky- family, heavy struggle, too much to carry, vulnerability, weak (2)
Hands- holding clutching, letting go, serving, receiving, giving (4)

Head- ideas, thinking, contains internal computer (6&7)
Heart- center of love and security, desires, acceptance (4)
Hips- balance, movement, strength (1&2)
Kidneys- filtering toxic emotions, letting go of the past (2)
Knee- stubborn, ego, pride, inability to give in, to bend, changing direction (1)
Legs- carrying us forward, standing up for yourself, motion (1)
Lips- words, speech, communicating freely (5)
Lungs- breathing in life, freedom, suffocating (4)
Mouth- nourishing yourself, speaking out (5)
Neck- flexibility, seeing all sides, tunnel vision (5)
Nose- self-recognition, nosiness, in front of your face (6)
Ovaries- creativity, feminine power, releasing and letting go, birthing ideas (2)
Prostate- masculine energy, virility (2)
Sciatica- burdens, dragging a heavy load, moving forward alone(1)
Shoulders- carrying lives burdens, lifting the load for others (5)
Sinus- stuffed unexpressed feelings need to cry, unable to breathe around others (6)
Skin- protection, sensitivity, being touched (4)
Solar plexus- intuition, gut feeling, emotional control center (3)
Spine- flexible, support, integrity, standing straight (1)
Stomach- digest ideas, nourishment, sustain self (3)
Teeth- words you speak, begins the process of digestion (5)
Testicles- masculinity, manhood (2)
Throat- expression, creativity, able to speak up for oneself, swallowing words (5)
Thymus- fear of fighting back, in need of protection, heart connection (4)
Thyroid- expressing what you want, making your voice known, speaking freely (5)
Toes- balance, mobility (1)
Tongue- taste, pleasure (5)
Tonsil- expression, emotional creativity (5)
Uterus- home of creativity, birthing your desires , nurturing your ideas(2)
Wrist- movement and ease, serving self (4)

Diseases

Acne- dislike of self, outbursts of anger, negative thoughts directed toward self
ADD/ADHD- in need of attention, ultra-sensitive to energy, environmental overload
Addictions- lack of love for self, running away, no confidence
Addison disease- emotional malnutrition, exhausted from life
Adenoids- family frictions, arguments
Allergies-full of toxic emotions, ultra sensitive to others emotions
Alzheimer's- pain in remembering, wanting to forget the past, fear of dying
Anorexia- not worthy of nourishment, need for control, starving to know oneself
Anxiety- unable to breathe for oneself, accumulated childhood stress, fear of fear
Arteriosclerosis- a build of negative emotions from the past, fear of letting go
Arthritis- critical, lack of love for self, pushing yourself too hard, inflamed relationships
Asthma- feeling suffocated, holding back tears, emotional stress in family

Back pain-in need of physical touch, feeling unsupported

Baldness- negative thinking, need to control, worrying

Bed wetting- Fear of parent, too much stored stress, needing release, unable to relax

Bladder infection- pissed off, unable to let old emotions go, holding on to anger

Blood pressure- flow of life

        Low- in need of joy and happiness, participating in life

        High- stopping the flow of life, shutting down, holding back emotions, sadness

Boils- explosive anger, negative thoughts, being hard on oneself

Bronchitis- lack of family communication, prolonged exposure to irritating circumstances

Bruises- moving too fast, unaware of hurting oneself, pain below the skin

Bruxism- holding back words, fear of being heard, biting your tongue

Bulimia- dislike of self, giving up on self, unworthiness, undeserving

Bursitis- repressed anger, unable to make moves for oneself

Cancer- unresolved emotional issues eating away at you, holding on to the past, anger

Canker sores- angry words held back, restricted communication

Carpal tunnel- pushing yourself when in pain, I am not worthy, receiving issues

Cataracts- afraid of seeing the future because of self-neglect to the body

Cellulite- holding on to toxic emotions, protecting oneself from others

Cholesterol- unable to live joyfully, built up negative emotions, restricting the flow of life

Cold sores- unable to communicate positively, negative words, gossip, angry words

Colitis- letting go of the past, involuntary release of past emotions

Constipation- holding on to past hurts, burying the past, unable to let it go and flow

Depression- issue overload, pushing down emotions that are too painful, low spirits

Diabetes- undeserving of the sweet taste of life, shattered expectations, afraid to dream

Diarrhea- not dealing with problems, the body's way of letting go of negative emotions

Earache- fighting in the home, angry words intolerable to listen to

Eczema- an emotional irritation that has gotten under the skin, itching to let it go

Edema- holding on to emotions, unable to cry

Emphysema-harsh restrictions from the past, unable to breathe freely, feeling suffocated

Eyes- seeing the movie of life, the window to the soul

 Far sighted- painful present, living in the future

 Near sighted- fear of the future, living in the past

Fat- armor over time, ultra sensitive to old hurts, protection, taking on other's issues

 Arms- protecting the heart, big hearted

 Abdomen- female issues of sexuality, emotional protection, asserting power

 Hips- family issues stored from the past, feminine presence

 Thighs- holding on to anger from the past, need to stand strong for oneself

Fibromyalgia-hurts, buttons pushed, deep-seated resentment, beating yourself up inside

Fibroid tumors and cysts- hurt from a sexual partner, holding on to anger

Gallstones- bitterness, hard thoughts unresolved, unable to digest old hurts

Gray hair- stress, worrying all the time

Heart attack- lack of joy in living, money and power are more important than love

Heart burn- unable to stomach heart felt situations, unable to digest angry emotions

Hernia- ruptures relationships from the past, pressure to let go

Kidney stones- unable to release past emotions, unfiltered waste, toxic emotions

Laryngitis- fear of speaking up for self, feeling unworthy of having a voice

Menstrual problems- rejecting femininity, emotional stress, unable to flow with life

Migraines- blocked memories, unable to see or deal with the past, sexual tension

Neck problems- not seeing all sides of the issue, unwilling to change, tunnel vision

Nosebleeds- crying for love and recognition, notice me

Osteoporosis- lack of support, fear of standing up for oneself, feeling weak

Overweight- in need of protection, wearing armor, world weighing on you

Pink eye- clouded vision, seeing through rose colored glasses

Premenstrual syndrome- feeling powerless in being a woman, needing time to oneself

Prostate problems- giving up sexually, feeling old, broken masculinity

Rheumatoid arthritis- eating away at oneself, critical, unable to move forward

Sinusitis- stuffed unexpressed feelings, need to cry, and irritation to someone close to you

Sore throat- unable to express oneself, holding back tears

Stuttering- fear of expressing oneself freely with a parent, needing to cry, stress

Sty- anger at someone close to you, who is irritating you? What do you not want to see?

Tinnitus- not hearing or listening to your inner voice

Tonsillitis- years of repressed self-expression

Tumors- old hurts accumulated over the years in need of release, in need of forgiveness

Ulcers- stress, unable to breathe, feeling suffocated, stored unexpressed tears or anger

These are only a few interpretations and, like in a good dream book, they represent individual metaphoric views and perceptions. After doing your own readings, you will see consistencies in the mind/body connection. Write down your own interpretations as if you are reading a dream. You will end up with your own intuitive explanations. Remember, everything means something; you are more like a spiritual detective than anything else. I feel that the universe is always speaking to us. Are we listening? You have to be conscious of every clue and be able to "plug" into the person who is picking the crystals. Having confidence in your intuition will help you help others. Asking the right questions and listening wholeheartedly will help you increase the accuracy of your readings. My crystals speak to me and over time, yours will too. Just have faith in your abilities.

Emotional Health and Thoughts – There is No Such Thing as Time

Our bodies respond to our thoughts - past, present, and immediate future. We may worry about the future, but the body thinks it is the present. It doesn't know the difference. Your body has experiences as your thoughts float across your mind. Your body can react with tension, excitement, and possibly even fear. Thinking negatively about the future only creates unnecessary stress in an already stressful world. If I had to come up with the most important factor affecting overall health, it would be **worrying** about the future. It hasn't even happened yet and we are wasting precious energy thinking negatively about it. If you are going to have the luxury of entertaining a thought, you might as well make it a good one. The term I use is "wish craft." Ask yourself how balanced your thoughts are between positive and negative wishes for your future. Worrying about your future is really just focusing on thoughts of bad things to come. It is like Glinda says in the Wizard of Oz, "Are you a good witch or a bad witch?" Thoughts are potentialities, cast into the ethereal world, representing what you would like to manifest in the physical world.

Another thing we do is relive the past and blame others for our lack of inner development. We have all been victimized in the past. What have you learned from that experience? Will you change yourself accordingly, so you will not pass the injustice on to the next generation? I believe that life is our training ground and we all showed up here to learn certain lessons. Ultimately, we are all in control of everything that happens to us in this lifetime, and all of our lifetimes to come. This idea puts us back in the driver's seat and abolishes victimization. You can take hold of your steering wheel and change the direction you are headed at any time. The choice is up to you.

" I just need to learn the depth of doubt or faith to fall into."-Collective Soul

Stress, Emotions and Dis-ease

I believe that stress and stored emotions can cause *dis-ease* within our bodies. Taking in positive healthy information feeds our spirits. However, watching stressful adrenalin-filled news programs, horror movies, or talk shows only accumulate negative energy like a virus, and we become garbage dumps of unwanted emotions and stress. If only we were born with a personal "firewall" already installed in our most precious computer: our mind. If you go back to the chakra prescriptions, you will notice that watching television, eating fast food and going to the mall are not on the list. Yet, that is a normal day for some people. Speeding home in traffic to watch the news and tuning out for the rest of the evening, only to do it again the very next day, isn't a healthy lifestyle. We wake up late and eat nothing, race off to work or school. Exhausted, we live on coffee and energy drinks, dissipating our energy to a catastrophically low level, leading to depression or what I call "low spirits." Low energy and high stress levels are the main causes of sickness in our society today, destroying our immune systems and playing havoc within the body's management systems, our chakras.

The stresses we aren't aware of accumulate and our metaphoric cup runith over! Consider irritable bowel syndrome (IBS). Over many years of readings, I have consistently found that those who have had traumatic experiences and have never been able to emote properly, tend to have this condition. Often, their bodies are "screaming" for them to talk to someone and release this energetic load. Their mind believes that no one will listen, or they have been told that they are not worthy of being heard. Their bodies can no longer store the issues. Adding more stress into this equation causes the body to remember the experiences that have piled up from the past; and creates an overload of emotional baggage. Could there be a metaphoric relationship between stress, emotional issues and physical incontinence?

Both our present and our past affect our current and future health. In your childhood, if you had someone that loved and supported you with whom you could talk and get things "off your chest," you most likely persevered through your many stressful experiences. If you have been made to feel unimportant and insignificant as a child, you may believe that you do not matter, and lack such fortitude. Children need loving environments to be healthy. If they grow up without loving supportive guidance, they may become diseased adults. Without it, these adults must take on the task of healing their past so they can live in the present. If these people do not appropriately process past pains and sufferings, then the negative experiences (energy) must be stored somewhere. Everyone has stuff! It is how we deal with our past emotional issues that make the difference between health and disease.

Obsessive-compulsive disorder (OCD) is another yet unexplained phenomenon. While many attempt to derive a physical cause for such a condition, others (myself included) believe it is more of an emotional issue. When we are younger and live in stress-filled homes, we act as sponges, soaking up the overloading experiences around us. Trying to control the chaos in the home, we take on more than we bargained for, absorbing everyone's troubles. In this case, we may feel unexplained emotions throughout our days, leaving us asking, "what is wrong with me?" It may be my mother's emotions, my father's, my sibling's, or is it a schoolmate's. At this point, our computer is on overload and we start to malfunction. Simple day-to-day life becomes unmanageable when we have reached our capacity for stress. The body reacts, and we start to break down internally, desperately trying to find some control in life. We clean our room until everything is in its place, we tap our pencil three times before tests and we wash our hands over and over again because these behaviors are within our control. I have also found that these individuals are often the most gifted and sensitive people, and have become truly misunderstood in society.

Quieting the minds of those who suffer from OCD and getting some release from their everyday stresses will help them unload "baggage" from their past. This release gives them back their control. What does all this have to do with Crystal Readings? In cases of OCD, you will find most of the stones will be in the sixth chakra and their favorite color will be purple. I find that most people with OCD are likely Indigo children and need a lot of tender loving care. They are overstimulated by TVs, computers, video games, outside electricity sources, diet, food additives, colorings, preservatives and environmental allergens. Helping them see their overly open sixth chakra can help them understand these sensitivities, allow them to become more balanced, and lead to an effective chakra prescription.

Another abbreviated *dis-ease* is ADD and ADHD. In ancient times, children who had these "disorders" would be considered seers, highly respected individuals who would go to special schools and were valued for their gift of intuition. After all, that is where foster care originated! Now these children are placed in crowded classrooms, only to end their day sitting in front of a television at daycare, or go home to sit in front of a video game, eating food cooked in a microwave oven, while talking for hours on their personal cell phones. A less toxic environment would help these gifted misunderstood children. Drugging them is not the answer. Parents and teachers who encourage individuality and self-expression help these children flourish, enabling them to maintain their spirit. Grounding exercises like yoga, tai chi, running and walking outdoors, pure diets and stress-free environments can truly benefit these children. Remember, everything is energy, even the food we eat. Compare a sit down, home-cooked meal with your family, to eating a high-fat hamburger with fries made by a teenager who hates their job. Can you see the energetic connection? Protecting our youth and feeding them positive energy in every aspect of their lives will pay off for all of us in the long run.

"Give an Indigo child who has been tagged as ADD or ADHD something to study that he or she is interested in, and you will see the brilliance unfold before your eyes. There is so much we need to learn in order to allow the great potential of these kids to come to light."
-Drunvalo Melchizede

Not long ago, I had been doing readings with a young girl, barely eight years old. I knew she was brilliant, possibly an indigo child. I also saw that she had a past life in the military. One of her problems in school was that she would only draw guns and bombs in black pencil. She would never use color, or choose more cheerful subjects. Her hair was cut very short and she had black circles under her eyes. She was overly concerned with our men being at war and wanted me to know that our president didn't care! Remember, this was an eight-year-old girl relaying this information to me. I had seen this pattern in children a couple of times before, and in each case, I felt the child was strongly affected by their past lives in the military. While the influences of this live can be powerful, we must also consider the effects of past lives as well. This latest reading had come at a time when she had been put on a lot of medication because she was uncontrollable at school. The stones she drew were all in the first and second chakras. Normally, she would draw crystals representing her 6th and 7th chakras, as most Indigo children do. I said, "It looks like you are definitely grounded today!" She said, "I am, how did you know?" She told me that while riding in the backseat of her mother's car her shoe had "accidentally" slipped off her foot and hit her mom in the back of the head, and now she was grounded! We discussed her diet that day, and she said she hadn't eaten anything. When the reading was finished, she asked me if I knew how many licks it took to get to the center of a tootsie pop. Wide eyed, she said "223!" Obviously she had eaten candy (sugar and dye), and nothing else, which explains the shoe incident in the car. After hearing this, her mom took her off sugar, colors and preservatives completely and made many more changes in their lifestyle.

Her mother had been doing readings and had experienced great results, and in the process, had stopped using all of her medications. She had been reading a lot of nutrition and self-help books on her own and called me one day for advice. She said that she felt better without her prescriptions, and she wanted my opinion on whether taking her daughter off of her own medicines was a good idea. She went further, saying that these drugs were so strong that her daughter couldn't sleep at night. I told her it would have to be her and her physician's decision. I NEVER have given advice on medication prescribed by physicians, not being one myself. However, I feel prescriptions that focus more on contorting one's moods to conform to the way some experts think you should be feeling are dangerous. I can say that 99% of those who came in for multiple readings will tell me that over time they just feel that they don't need them anymore. The mother made the decision to take her daughter to see a naturopathic physician. The same young lady is now a pig-tailed cheerleader and the latest picture she drew for me was more colorful than many I had seen, a picture of an Angel. She even gave me an Antarctica Angel (Archangel) I keep it in my helpful people corner in my office (Feng Shui), she has helped me to better understand this phenomenon. Her mom continues to educate herself and now is going to massage school, delving into natural cures for her and her children.

"The doctor of the future will give no medicine but will interest his patients in the care of the human frame, in diet and in the cause and prevention of disease." -Thomas Edison

Special Prescriptions: Feng Shui

We've discussed the effects of holding onto emotions and experiences without an opportunity to clean out your closet, how this reveals itself in readings, and the logical chakra prescriptions that follow. A cluttered mind, and a few blocked chakras can also manifest chaos and disorder around the home. After all, the state of your home is a reflection of the state of your mind. These cases are opportunities for you to give a very special and powerful prescription using Feng Shui.

Feng Shui (pronounced "fung shway") - meaning wind and water - is an ancient Chinese art of placement and design, facilitating balance of energy (chi) in any given space. It is the study of how to arrange your outer world to enhance your inner world, by observing the relationship between seen and unseen forces. Remember, all thoughts are things, and your intentions are like prayers guiding the universe to help you initiate positive change. There are two very different uses of Feng Shui: clearing out your clutter, and what I call "praying in reverse," by moving your outer world to change your inner world, changing your mind in the process!

Clearing Your Head by Clearing Out Your Clutter

Our external world is a reflection of our internal state, and vice versa. This reciprocal circle can lead to cycles of chaos for those of you with your sixth and seventh chakras in disarray. Take a look around, do you feel confused by the amount of clutter falling in on you when you're at home? Many of your participants will resonate with this experience. The perfect prescription for such issues is a good old fashion housecleaning. Purging, in this sense, is truly therapeutic.

It is easy to instruct your participants on how to "clean house." Be organized and keep it simple. To begin, make sure you have your home free of dust and dirt. Get rid of anything that you do not love, especially anything that has bad memories from your past. Learn to let them go.

Don't expect to be able to clear your entire home in one session. In fact, many of my clients simply get rid of a bag of unwanted clutter once a week. Certain areas of your home have specific meanings attached to them in the larger Feng Shui scheme of things. This is called the bagua. Choose one area to work on, in order of importance. For example, if you're looking for a new job, cleanse your career corner first, then move on to your skills and knowledge area, and finally go over your prosperity corner. If you want to have children, work on your relationship corner first, then turn your attention to the children area, and finally take a look at your family area.

I had a reading with a woman who wanted to work on her prosperity corner and thought if her husband could sell some of the things he had stored in their garage, they would have some extra money. She was also convinced her husband needed to let go of some issues from his past. I turned it around and asked her if there was something *she* was holding onto metaphorically (remember the mirror technique), and she responded, by saying she had $5,000 of unopened crystal-ware she use to sell, in her bedroom closet. Not surprisingly, she also seemed to be holding onto some extra weight and wanted to work on her health. The prescription was easy to come up with in this case. Cleaning out our closets, storage units and homes allow us to lighten up energetically, and this will have physical effects as well.

If I see too many crystals in the lower chakras, the reading points to issues in the physical world. hen the same situation occurs in the upper chakras, I see the problem being too many thoughts and ideas unable to be manifested. Interestingly, these have correspondences to areas in your home. Garages and closets represent the lower chakras and attics represent the upper chakras. Cleaning out basements and working with the center of the home, representing health, can help weight issues.

When cleaning out your home, pick up one item at a time, look at it, and then feel what it represents. If you look at something and an unhealthy memory passes through your mind, let that object go! If it feels good, keep it and incorporate it in the area of the bagua that suits it. Metaphorically, you are telling the universe that you are open to receiving good in your life, and that you don't want anything negative coming your way. Feng Shui works well with Crystal Readings because it is an exercise in manifesting what we want. Asking for these things allows us to open our crown chakra. Focusing on what we want is the task of our third eye, our sixth chakra. Deserving what we ask for involves the heart and throat chakras. Finally, moving our stuff sends energy to the lower three chakras. It all starts with knowing what you want to manifest and translating this to a physical version of a prayer. That is the power of Feng Shui!

Praying in Reverse

I've already discussed manifesting things in the outer world by beginning with a thought and "birthing" it through your chakra system into the outer world. Thus, one can say that, an effect in your outer world is caused by forces in your inner world. Now, what about the reverse? Can forces in your outer world manifest changes in your inner world? Clearly, yes. We've already discussed influences on your energy system such as nutrition, people who you "plant" in your garden, and experiences you choose. The fact is, there are many ways to arrange your world and your experiences to have the desired effects within your chakras.

Feng Shui is the art of moving the tangible to change the intangible. If my intentions (prayers) are to have more abundance in my life, I will light a candle in my prosperity corner. If I want a healthier relationship with my spouse, I may buy two red roses and place them in my relationship corner. If, in a reading, I see that my participant's crown chakra is closed, I have them write down five things they would like to manifest in the years to come. They will usually come up with three things quickly then stop at four or five, I make them continue because as I know 5 in numerology represents change and that is what we want to do, to have the courage to mix our lives up a bit to get some momentum for some positive change. If I see that they have some blocks throughout their chakra system, I will prescribe cleaning out some of their past clutter by using Feng Shui. They usually start with one corner by prioritizing the most important issue they are having difficulties with at the time of their reading. By taking action in the material world and intentionally clearing your home of clutter you are metaphorically telling the universe that you have changed your mind! I call this "praying in reverse."

"You will never change your life unless you change something you do daily."
-Saul Bellow

The Bagua

The bagua is the shape of an octagon. There are nine areas in the bagua that you can choose to enhance. The front door of the home is located at the bottom of the bagua. Remember to let go of the old to make way for the new. Then enhace the corner of the bagua (your home) or the chakra that needs the most help.

Family: located at the left side of the octagon/bagua
Healthy plants, flowers, family heirlooms with good memories, furniture made of wood, family photos and the color green (2nd chakra)

Prosperity: located at the left upper corner of the octagon/bagua
Gold candle sticks, red candles, waterfall flowing into the bagua, an amethyst stone, jade plants, pictures of wealth and money and the color purple (1st and 3rd chakras)

Fame and Reputation: located directly across from the front door
Pointed objects, stars, pictures of famous people you admire, lights, fire, candles and the color red (3rd chakra)

Love and Relationships: located at the far right corner of the octagon/bagua
Artwork portraying romance and love, pairs, such as candlesticks, flowers, books and statues, mementos of love and the color pink (2nd and 4th chakras)

Children and Creativity: located at the right side of the octagon/bagua
Stuffed animals, children's artwork in metal frames, candy, games, music, round items, metal table and white objects (2nd and 5th chakras)

Helpful People and Travel: located at the nearest right corner of the octagon/bagua
Angels, deities, places you would like to travel to, pictures of people you look up to, silver and grey (1st, 2nd, 3rd and 7th chakras)

Career: located at the front door at the bottom of the octagon/bagua
Books on your desired profession, diplomas, job related awards, water, vases, fish bowls, black and white items (1st, 3rd and 7th chakras)

Skills and Knowledge: located at the nearest left corner of the octagon/bagua
Wise beings, dolphins, wizards and scholars, books that have helped you gain important knowledge and the color blue (3rd, 5th, 6th and 7th chakras)

Health: located in the middle of the octagon/bagua
Earth, healthy plants, stars, sunshine, crystals and the color yellow (All chakras)

My Daughter's Mind/Body Connection Feng Shui Story

At the age of nine, my daughter was thrown into the middle of a horrible divorce. Two years later she had gained 50 pounds, most of it above her waistline. She revealed later, that the divorce was eating her up inside, and to ease the pain, she had turned to food. A beautiful little girl with the biggest heart, she had become our little sponge and mediator. She called it the *middle child syndrome*, and she joked that she was Jan Brady, the middle daughter in the Brady Bunch. She even created a pretend boyfriend, named George Glass, as Jan had in an episode of the show. Her George Glass was a smiley-face balloon connected to a pillow body.

During the divorce she was forced to see a court-appointed counselor who did more harm than good. Finally, she got a break when the court ruled that she no longer had to attend visitations on the weekends. Emotionally relieved and able to be herself, she started slowly losing weight by riding the stationary bike, carrying water in her back- pack, and eating a healthier diet. Frustrated at first with lack of visible results, I assured her that she was building muscle and that over time her exercise would pay off. She kept at it, and within three months she was riding a half hour a day and feeling stronger and healthier. In high school she made the cheer squad two years running, epitomizing the word spirit and transforming the typical stereotype of a *cheerleader*!

During this time, I was perfecting my Crystal Readings and would practice on my family. The results were truly inspiring. During a reading with my daughter, I saw that her heart chakra was closed. This alarmed me; she had always been the girl with the big heart. We worked through this problem with a technique I call "time travel." I took her back to a time she felt she needed to protect her heart. She recalled the pain and embarrassment she felt, at age eleven, when she had been teased about her extra large gym shorts. As a result, she had shut down her most beautiful asset — her heart — to protect herself from the pain. I then guided her forward, and asked my daughter what this younger version of her had taught her. She saw that what she learned during that time could actually be a gift. That gift had been her acceptance of people and their differences. When we were done with the session, her chakra prescription was to find a picture of her open hearted self at age eleven, frame it, and put it in her relationship corner in her bedroom, thereby letting the universe know that she loved and wanted a relationship with her younger self. This allowed her to reopen her heart and to be whole again.

That year in school, she was required to do a senior project for graduation. She chose the mind-body connection and hands on healing (Reiki) as her topics. She spoke about her weight issue as a child and what it had taught her. She explained how our emotions affect us and how unaware we are of this mind/body connection. She opened up others to subjects such as energy and the chakras, by explaining how Reiki works. Her speech was wonderful and at times brought tears to my eyes. That year my daughter grew emotionally and spiritually and we watched that energy spill over into her academic life as well as to other endeavors. However, one question went unanswered for her: "why hadn't boys noticed her?" I knew why. I suggested that it was time to take the picture of her eleven-year-old self out of her relationship corner in her bedroom. For one thing, there was only one person in the picture. That says to the universe, "I want to be alone." Instead, I had bought her a statue of a dancing couple at Christmas, but hesitated to give it to her until after graduation (she was getting good grades and hanging around with us on Saturday nights, it was a blessing).

We replaced her 11-year-old picture with the swing dancing couple, where the man was actually a soldier in the WWII era. We also bought two heart candles and two flowers: one pink and one blue, placing them in the same area. She wrote down her intentions and let them go. Her birthday was in June. She turned 18 and at her birthday party she received, yet again, another George Glass fake balloon guy. I told her she would have to say goodbye to George and her middle child syndrome from the Jan Brady days, and by destroying a George Glass piñata effigy. She did just that.

That same month, I had signed my kids up at my gym for free because of a promotional phone call I received, from whom we still don't know. The kids went alone one day and my daughter came home beaming. A boy had asked her out at the gym. He had on blue flowered Hawaiian shorts, and that day she was wearing the same, only pink (the pink and blue flowers). By July 4th we're having dinner with this young man, named Brady (the Brady Bunch). The synchronicities were overwhelming, and they kept coming.

Brady, who does up-close magic, performed his first trick with a deck of cards totally consisting of 4's, his favorite number…everyone who knows me knows that four is my favorite cosmic number! At dinner that night, he explained that he wanted to join the army, but because of the "Private Ryan Rule" he couldn't (the dancing couple statue). Brady later had a reading with me, which revealed that he and my daughter had both grown up learning lessons through some tough experiences. He had always been shy and afraid to talk or smile because his teeth were not well taken care of when he was younger. He told me it was hard to open up conversation with my daughter because of his teeth. His reading pointed to the energy in his throat chakra being closed. He opened his throat chakra in our reading by talking with me about his past. He also wrote down his future intentions about wanting to be a magician and being able to afford braces. Amazingly enough, the last card he chose in his reading was the *magician*, I even received a high-five with that card! Brady eventually got braces and is on his way to opening up heartfelt communication with the people in his life. Both he and my daughter have been given a gift… acceptance of another based on their inner self and not their outer appearance.

"Only as high as I reach can I grow, only as far as I seek can I go, only as deep as I look can I see, only as much as I dream can I be." -Karen Raven

Previously, I discussed the "jig-saw" phenomenon of people who are attracted to one another because of the complimentary nature of each person's traits. While this is often the case in relationships, it doesn't tell the whole story. In order to manifest a relationship with someone who has strengths which you may be lacking, one must at least have the intention of positive change underneath the surface. The law of attraction says, "like attracts like" we can only manifest into our lives what we already have within ourselves. If you want to attract positive change, then choose to do one thing different. On the other hand, if you are happy with they way your life is going, then keep doing what works for you. Most of the people I have done readings with want change in at least one area of their lives. In fact, to focus on encouraging positive change in one particular area of your life at a time is a great idea. I use the term "fuel tanks" to describe this. No one can work on every aspect of their life at once. At any time, certain fuel tanks that you have will be full, and certain ones will be almost empty. No one has the perfect life. If money is flowing in, then that tank is full. However, I may choose to work on my health if I have gained a few pounds. If my relationships are going well, I can work on my career. I seem to be working on one or two areas at all times. While writing this book, I have worked on my *skills and knowledge* and *helpful people*. Before that, I was working on prosperity, family and relationships, I change tanks when one becomes full and another needs topping off. Feng Shui is a fun and easy way to encourage positive changes. Ultimately, it is a wonderful way to remember how to open up your crown chakra, remind the universe of your heartfelt intentions and pray for the most important person in your life, you. After all this is your life to LIVE!

My Story of Intention

Years ago, I asked the woman who worked at my favorite bookstore for something totally new. She gave me my first book on Feng Shui. After reading it, I found it interesting and put it away for a year. The second time I read it, though, I thought I would give Feng Shui a try. I began with my prosperity corner. I purchased a fountain, some green candles and bought a large amethyst and placed them in my prosperity corner. Months later, I unexpectedly came into $9,000, and I was thrilled. Being a single mother of three, I decided to try it on my relationship corner in my bedroom. I cleaned out the mold and dust, threw away the broken mirror and got rid of the pictures of lonely women surrounded by Angels by my bed. I went to the craft shop and bought a picture called *The Accolade* (where a princess is knighting her knight), red candles, a heart crystal and a Book entitled *Enchanted Love* by Marianne Williamson. In the months following, I lit the candles and read the book. That year, I learned to date and have a relationship with the most exciting person I knew… myself! Eight months later I met a man at an event I would normally go to alone and we have been together ever since.

Three months after seeing each other, I went to his home to discover that he had also bought *The Accolade*, at approximately the same time that I had, and for Christmas that year, he bought me the book called *A Womans Worth* by Marianne Williamson. We are now married and his picture (much larger then mine) is in our relationship corner in our bedroom. My *Accolade* now hangs in the relationship corner of my office, as a constant reminder that when you set your intentions, the universe steps in and gives you what your heart truly desires.

"I thought you would never get here, I said. I know. That is what took me so long."
-Marianne Williamson *Enchanted Love*

During the phase of combining our finacial papers I came across my husband's old receipts (he is a packrat but is becoming enlightened gradually). Interestingly, I came across the old receipt for *The Accolade*. Other pictures he purchased that day were *Celestial Planetarium, Father and Child* and *Dream House*. I have been following the stars for years and my favorite number is 4. The total that day was $144. The day of our wedding, my son gave a speech that brought tears to our eyes about his new father. We are in the process of looking for our dream home. When you learn how to follow the stars the synchronicities just keep coming!

Love 101 and I AM Worthy

Before I really loved myself, my readings all pointed to me living in the clouds. When I drew my crystals they were always purple amethysts, clear quartz crystals and blue aquamarine. I was full of inspiration, intuition and creativity but never going anywhere with my ideas. My core issue was understanding my own self worth and deservedness (heart chakra). I could give to others but not to myself. I remember writing on a piece of paper (fifth chakra) everything that I desired in a relationship and then putting it away. At night, I would visualize a faceless man who wore a tie, pampered me and lived with me in my dream house on a lake. I knew the essence of what I wanted and spent years daydreaming about it in my mind's eye (sixth chakra). That was as far as I could go with my vision because my energy was blocked at my heart chakra... I didn't truly feel that I was worthy of such a man. The potential was there for me to manifest my soulmate, but was stuck in an ethereal limbo in my head. I needed to love myself first to manifest my hearfelt intentions into a physical form. I looked at my list and realized that I was missing half of what I wanted from my soulmate. I spent a year cultivating the things on my list and nurturing myself (third and second chakra). I dated myself as if I was the goddess I knew myself to be inside. I bought myself roses weekly, exercised, took long baths and spent quality time with myself going places I used to want a man to take me. I even learned to dance alone, and feel great while doing it. I was learning to have the best time of my life, with me. I also dated my kids one at at time, fixed up my home and realized how blessed my life truly was. The moment I realized I was happy and comfortable with me, was the day I met my soulmate.

Remember to ask for what you want and let it go. Visualize your intentions as if you already have them. Write them down and talk about your ideas and aspirations. Feel open to receiving from your core being and be thankful for all that you have in your life now. Have a gratitude attitude. Take action towards achieving your hopes and dreams. Seek out and surround yourself with others who will support and encourage you in your vision and when you manifest what you have visualized, remember to tell the universe "thank you!" Before you know it, all of your lofty inspired thoughts will magically come to fruition right before your very eyes and you too, will be experiencing heaven on earth.

"We are what we think. All that we are arises from our thoughts.
With our thoughts we make the world."-Buddha

Afterword

When I began writing this book, I believed it would be a short booklet on the *how-to*'s of Crystal Readings. I had a few friends and family members read it to help edit some changes. In the process, it changed them - just a little at first, then in leaps and bounds. My booklet is now a full-length book, and this is a new beginning for me. I hope to teach my art, and through it, help others empower themselves. I hope the words in this book encourage you to do something different in your life, taking you to the next level in the chakra system: from surviving to thriving!

I started this book to fill up the many hours that I waited for clients to appear at my door. The Angels told me to write, and so I did. At first, I had no idea how to use a computer, so I asked my daughter to help. We got through the Astrological part, and like an Aries, she was off to start something new. I was left alone to fend for myself, and fend for myself I did. This not only made the endeavor truly mine, but it gave me a new talent of using spell check and CTRL-Z. I loved writing and most of my computer metaphors found in this book were from my new experiences: data-dumping, viruses and firewalls. We treat our computers with more respect than we do our own minds, and then we wonder where all the *dis-ease* comes from in our bodies. As the stories from my clients piled up, I combined the knowledge from all the wonderful books that I have read over the last twenty years with many real-life wonderful readings.

If I had any advice to give you to encourage personal growth, it would be to read a book on anything that lifts your spirits. Then, store your newly acquired uplifting knowledge in your own personal computer: your mind. I have so many books, that I send one home with each one of my clients. Following a reading, one book in particular usually sticks out, and I send it home with them. Some clients read the books, and others return them apologizing, "I didn't have the time." The people who read the books make the greatest gains. I call it "positive brainwashing." Reading something great and meaningful fills your mind with life-affirming energy. I read something every day to keep my spirits high. I have many Angel books with short encouraging paragraphs that say, "you can do it," just enough to keep me going in a positive direction. I rarely get that same encouragement from the T.V. or the newspaper. The books I read say that I am okay, and that I am good enough. Those words may not ring true at first, but one day you'll start to accept yourself, and eventually you'll act on it. It is that whole self-love idea…it really works! I learned years ago that if you wait around for someone else to give you the approval or positive attention that you need, you could be waiting a long, long, time.

This year at Christmas I was the nice Grinch whose heart "grew three sizes that day" (the end of the story). The experience really reminded me how important an open heart chakra is for over all health. I went about town each day over Christmas vacation, giving small gifts to adults that I didn't know. To see each person accept a gift, wrapped in 'heart' paper, was a study in itself. Some refused, while others lit up like a star! The ones that refused had shut their hearts down years ago, and had no intention of going back. Others took a chance maintaining an open heart, risking the pain and all that it entails. These were also the people who were open to the many joys of life. I gave out colored crayons and markers, and told them to get in touch with their child-like spirits by using their presents in the next twenty-four hours. I now have a picture of a Christmas tree topped with a star in my office… colored by a 65 year old man!

After playing the Grinch (with the big heart), I recognized the slow death we put our spirits through when we stop feeling, by creating a huge chakra block laying smack dab in the middle of our chakra systems – in our hearts. That same holiday season, I watched this slow process at my son's basketball game. There was a little girl around five-years-old twirling, skipping and dancing around the court while the game was going on. I told her mother "with a little more of that in the world, there would be no more wars." A minute later, she ran to the other side of the bleachers, and in seconds, the same little girl had tears running down her cheeks. The kind we used to cry before the world told us that it isn't OK to freely emote! When I saw her running back to her mother, I had to know what happened. It seemed the man on the other side of the bleachers was her father, and the two parents must be divorced or separated. The father obviously scolded the girl for something. Eventually the little girl returned to dancing and twirling, but in my mind I thought, "I bet she said 'I'm not going to do that again'." Those small thoughts turn our hearts down a notch, desensitizing us to our own feelings. How many more times does it have to happen before she stops feeling, twirling and dancing? In that moment I realized that the universe had revealed my purpose. To help others re-open their heart chakras… "Open-heart surgery" in a spiritual sense, to encourage others to allow their energy to flow through all of their chakras. This is how that booklet turned into this book!

Love and Heartfelt Light,
Dena Marie

"The release of atom power has changed everything except our way of thinking…
The solution to this problem lies in the **heart of mankind.** If only I had known,
I should have become a watchmaker." –Albert Einstein

The Books That Changed My Life

Colors and Chakras
Wheel of Life
Anodea Judith, Ph.D.

The Seven-Fold Journey
Anodea Judith, Ph.D. and Selene Vega

The Book of Chakras
Ambika Wauters

Feminine Energy
The Divine Feminine
Margaret Starbird

Crystals
The Crystal Bible
Judy Hall

Astrology
The Only Astrology Book You Will Ever Need
Joanne Martin Woolfolk

Numerology
The Life You Were Born to Live
Dan Millman

Colors and Numbers
Louise L. Hay

Dreams
The Mystical Magical Marvelous World of Dreams
Wilda B. Tanner

Feng Shui
Move Your Stuff, Change Your Life
Karen Rauch Carte

Intuition
Trust Your Vibes
Sonia Choquette

Inspiration
The Power of Intention
Wayne Dyer

Mind and Body
You Can Heal Your Life
Louise L. Hay

The Science of Medical Intuition
Caroline Myss and Norm Shealy, M.D.

Feelings Buried Alive Never Die
Karol K. Truman

Prescription for Nutritional Healing
James F. Balch and Phyllis A. Balch, C.N.C

Personal Growth
A Return to Love
Marianne Williamson

Radical Forgiveness
Colin Tippery

In the Meantime
Iyanla Vanzant

Be Your Own Guru
Betty Bethards

The Miracle of Mindfulness
Thich Nhat Hanh

The cards I use in my Crystal Readings are:

The Voyager Tarot
James Wanless, Ph.D.
www.voyagertarot.com

Archangel Oracle Cards
Doreen Virtue, Ph.D.

My Own Journey

As a personal fitness trainer for more than fourteen years, my career focused on helping people overcome issues such as weight gain, low self-esteem, and motivation through the medium of physical exercise. However, my experiences in the fitness industry gradually revealed that these issues, and many others, manifest themselves not only from inadequate physical conditioning, but also from unhealthy mental and emotional states. I discovered that clients whose self-esteem was high received longer-lasting results than those who felt poorly about themselves. This observation led me to move from simply training the physical body to helping my clients also nurture a healthy mind and spirit. My journey and many synchronicities led me in the direction of hypnotherapy, working with the power of the mind and using Reiki to assist in the spiritual/energetic realm of healing. I have combined the two, and now think of myself as an *Energetic Counselor*. As in personal training, every client's therapy is unique, tailored to their needs and perceptions. I use this philosophy, combined with an intuitive approach to healing, to usher my clients to the destinations they seek. Spiritual communication plays a major role in my diverse range of counseling techniques; Crystal Readings, Light Touch Therapy Treatments, Coupling Therapy and Chakra Prescriptions. As the world moves toward healing its pain instead of masking it, I envision myself evolving with new techniques, blossoming with deeper insights, and empowering others to venture on their own personal journeys back to wholeness.

For more information on:

- Copies of this book
- Crystal Starter Kits
- Enhancement Kits
- Crystal Reading Workshops
- Personal Consultations
- Speaking Engagements
- Other works by Dena Marie

Go to:
www.dena-marie.com

…or write to us at:

Lift Your Spirits
PO Box 1442
Snohomish, WA 98290

If you have had successes using the information in my book, and want to share those experiences with others, please email me your stories at: ourstories@dena-marie.com.

**"And in the end… the love you take,
is equal to the love you make."-The Beatles**